D1385135

THE ART OF FIXING THINGS

Principles of machines
and how to repair them
OVER 150
tips and tricks
to make things last longer
and save you money

Three generations of self reliant people have contributed to this book. The first was my great-grandfather, Nathanial Pierce, who died before I was born. The second was my father, Charles Pierce, and the third is me.

Many of the tips in this book come to you from 90 or 100 years ago. Some things may change over time, but one thing is for sure: since the invention of the consumer economy, there will always be someone who will try to make more money by cutting back on quality.

This book is dedicated to my father, Charles Harrison Pierce, 1916–1996.

1955, London, working as an Engineer for TWA.

Published by Lawrence E. Pierce, Box 82, Hornby Island BC Canada V0R 1Z0

WWW.THEARTOFFIXINGTHINGS.COM

Photo illustrations by Margit Lieder

Layout and cover design by Adrian Horvath // adrianhorvath.net

The author wishes to thank Margit for all her hard work with the red pen. Her years of teaching ESL at Killarney High School prepared her for my errors. However, sometimes I did not take her advice.

I also wish to thank Andrea Eder for lending a helping hand, and nose to this project.

CONTENTS

APPLIANCE // HOUSEHOLD // GARDEN

Get a chainsaw and seriously save money	TIP // 055
Putting rubber belts back on	TIP // 056
Holding two or more wires together easily	TIP // 057
Repair a garden hose	TIP // 058
Electrical tape	TIP // 059
Bicycles	TIP // 060
Wall anchors	TIP // 061
Clean up that steam iron that you melted stuff on	TIP // 062
Sharpening scissors	TIP // 63
Outsmart cheap Chinese made lamps	TIP // 064
Sharpening blender blades	TIP // 065
Sharpening lawn mower blades	TIP // 066
Oil that sewing machine	TIP // 067
Practice breaking things	TIP // 0068
Unscrewing things	TIP // 069
Appliance problems	TIP // 070
Grease your appliances	TIP // 071
Re-new electrical connections	TIP // 072
Belt dressing and belt adjustment	TIP // 073

Start that lawn mower or tiller first pull	TIP // 074
Buying the best appliances at the best prices	TIP // 075
Replacing a plug on a household appliance	TIP // 076
Buying parts	TIP // 077

GENERAL

Removing something that is pressed onto a shaft	TIP // 078
Making a neat punched hole	TIP // 079
Selecting the right size drill bit for a wood screw	TIP // 080
Using two hammers at once	TIP // 081
Use your nose	TIP // 082
Read the manual	TIP // 083
Know when you are in over your head	TIP // 084
Easy removal of stuck rubber hoses	TIP // 085
Grease everything	TIP // 086
Increase the power of your hand tools	TIP // 087
How to use heat to help take things apart	TIP // 088
Using a cold chisel to remove nuts	TIP // 089
Unscrewing something is not a one way street	TIP // 090
Using a nut to take hammer blows on end of shaft/bolt	TIP // 0091
Make a tool to repair damaged threads	TIP // 092

Another way to repair damaged threads	TIP // 093
Use a socket to install a seal	TIP // 094
Magic liquid that makes everything work better	TIP // 095
Save your knuckles	TIP // 096
The problem you cannot solve	TIP // 097
Wire brush threads	TIP // 098
The part that will go on two different ways	TIP // 099
Locking threaded things	TIP // 100
Understanding threads	TIP // 101
Strength of nuts and bolts	TIP // 102
Getting a nut into an impossible spot	TIP // 103
Making fittings leak proof	TIP // 104
Aligning parts so you can bolt them together	TIP // 105
Wiggle it	TIP // 106
Proper washer pile ups	TIP // 107
Use a punch to drive things out	TIP // 108
Selecting the right size drill bit for a machine bolt	TIP // 109
Take it apart so you can put it back together again	TIP // 110
Always put hardware in containers	TIP // 111
Loosening threads	TIP // 112

INTRODUCTION

This book shows you over 150 useful ideas you can use to fix things, save money, and impress your spouse. Repairing something that is broken is a true accomplishment, and is far more satisfying that just buying a new one.

This hands on Guide is based on my 55 years experience fixing things, as a professional mechanic, home handyman, and farmer.

I learned many things from my father, a do-it-yourselfer, who survived the last Depression. He was raised by his grandfather, Nathanial Pierce, in York, Nebraska. My great-grand father was another do-it-yourselfer. The 1930's was a time when repairing things was common. Buying a new one was not an option for many families.

I started at age 9 with a mechanical wind up alarm clock. I found it had a broken main spring. I fixed it.

Today, most companies that make things, want us to throw them away, when they stop working, and buy new ones. Some brands are not so much about quality as they are about mass marketing. Many "brand names" do not even own factories, they just contract for the production of goods with the lowest bidder in China.

Many things made in China cannot be fixed, but many other things can be, if you know the basics. Often the companies who make fixable things, would prefer that you throw them away.

The constant drain of replacing consumer goods has led to bigger family debt, and bigger national debt, including, in the United States, a staggering trade deficit with China. In May 2011, China held $1.16 Trillion in U.S. Treasuries, making them the biggest creditor of the United States. Jobs flowing to China means more unemployment at home. A vicious cycle is repeated every time you buy a Chinese, or other, product, that cannot be repaired.

If you can squeeze just one extra year out of your car, you will have saved thousands of dollars. Squeeze another 4 years out of major appliances, and you will save hundreds. By doing this, you will be better off, and so will your country.

Things used to last way longer than 3 years. This Guide will help you fix appliances, cars, and garden machines. There are also a few tips on wood working.

This Guide is not about any particular car, appliance, or piece of machinery. It is about all of them. Although some specific repairs are illustrated, this book contains general ideas for repairing machinery and appliances of all sorts, and generally making things last longer.

When something breaks, you risk nothing by taking it apart to see if it can be fixed.

These are the tricks that are rarely, if ever written about. Most of them are not part of any car repair book, appliance repair guide, or on-line forum. This Guide provides the most complete advice available.

You should always search YouTube and Google for your particular problem, and consider what is on line, along with the advice in this Guide.

The art of fixing things is almost lost, and I hope to help revive it, before China gets the rest of our money, and jobs.

. . . .

LIABILITY WARNING

Here is the obvious stuff: gasoline, paint thinner, propane, solvent, and other flammable things, will explode/burn, probably give rats cancer, and hurt you, and/or destroy your property. Metal things can hurt you, sharp things can cut you. AC current (household electricity) can kill you. Battery acid can burn you, blind you, wreck your clothes.

If you venture out of bed you can get hurt, and if you do anything mentioned in this book, you can hurt or kill yourself, or damage your property, or the property of others.

Preferably, DO NOT READ ANY FURTHER.

If this WARNING scares you, send this book back RIGHT NOW for a refund. Do not copy it. We take absolutely no responsibility for you, your wife, heirs, kids, siblings, or personal property.

My lawyer said I had to tell you all this, so you would not even think about suing me when you drop that lawnmower engine on your foot, stick that running chain saw bar into your knee, or split a knuckle open, and need a Band Aid.

SAFETY

I am old school, and do not use rubber gloves when working on machines.

Waterless hand cleaner is way cheaper and more convenient than rubber gloves.

However, light weight surgical gloves for working on cars seem to be very popular.

Over the years I have become much more sensitive to automotive liquids. Gasoline, some gear oil, and some grease, make me feel terrible. It makes my joints hurt for 24 to 36 hours, and really messes up my sleep.

So there is something in some products that is not healthy on the skin, or in your lungs. Be warned.

Wear safety glasses. I never did, but I have prescription glasses, and they have accumulated a lot of pitting from flying objects.

Never crawl under your car while on a jack, unless there is some indestructible object, like a large piece of wood, axle stand, or Superman, that will catch the car if the jack slips or breaks.

Do not work on household electrical devices, unless they are unplugged.

The information about household electricity contained in this book relates to North America ONLY. If you are in any other part of the world get local advice.

THE
BASICS

· ·

When I bought my first laptop, in 1993, the instructions said to "Reboot" the computer in the event of certain problems. So, I went to the Index, and the Table of Contents, and to my dismay, there was no mention of "Reboot." I had no idea what that term meant.

I suspect many of the readers of this Guide will be as unfamiliar with certain basic terms, tools, and tool uses, as I was with "Reboot".

Here are the basics on using tools.

· ·

Push down to tighten

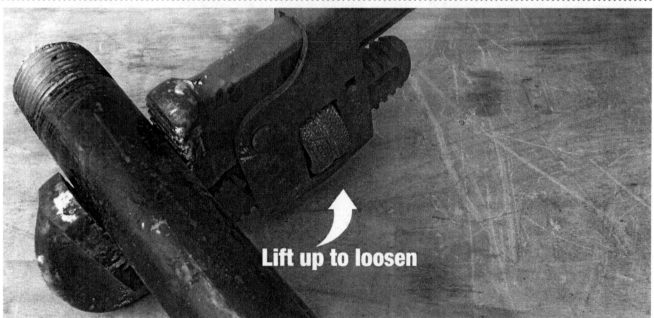

Lift up to loosen

PIPE WRENCH

001

It gets tighter as you turn the fitting, or pipe. The
jaws have teeth (I guess that is why they are called
"jaws")which bite into the pipe, or fitting.

It can be used on PVC water line fittings as well.

It only tightens one way, so turn it over to unscrew
something.

002 ▷ CRESCENT WRENCH

An adjustable wrench that will fit many sizes of nuts, bolts. Use the thumb wheel to set the size. As you turn a nut or bolt with this wrench, adjust the jaws with every turn, to avoid rounding the flat surfaces

Not good for all jobs, because the jaws are so wide, and it is hard to get it into tight places.

THE GRINDER

This tool will cut, smooth and shape metal. There are different disks for different uses, with different sizes. Ask your hardware store guy. You cannot do without it.

TIP | 004 | CHANNEL LOCK PLIERS

These adjustable pliers are good for grabbing large and small objects, and holding them.

Pictured are channel lock type pliers. Channel Lock is a brand name for pliers made in the USA. They must have made them first. Their web site says "Fiercely Made in Meadville PA." Sounds tough.

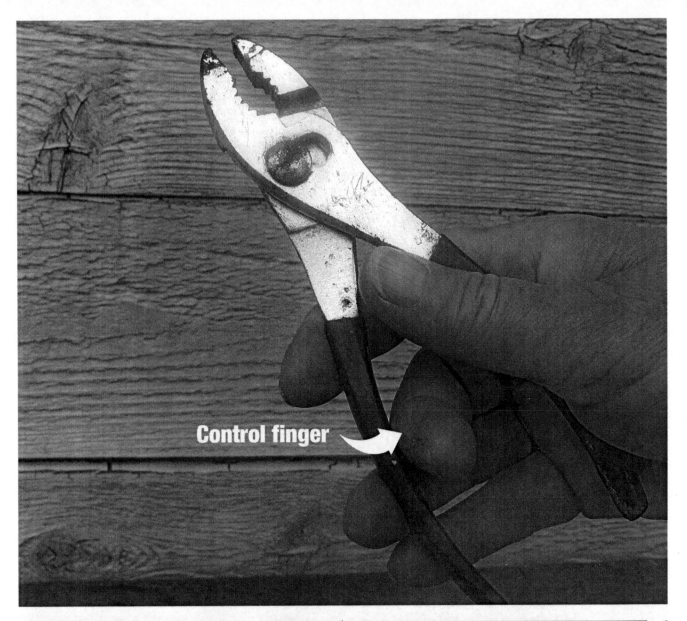

Control finger

USING PLIERS, WIRE CUTTERS, OR SIDE CUTTERS

Place one finger inside the two handles, so that you can open the tool, and close it with more accuracy.

Most cutting power here

006 ▷ **CUTTING WITH WIRE CUTTERS AND SIDE CUTTERS**

The greatest cutting force is where the jaws meet,
when wide open.

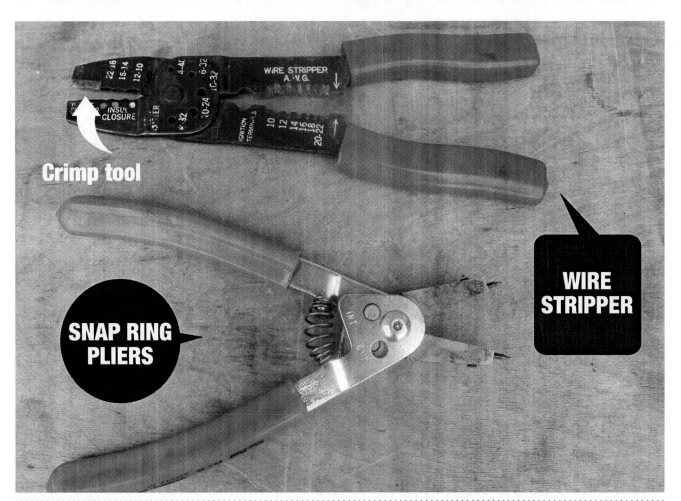

Crimp tool

SNAP RING PLIERS

WIRE STRIPPER

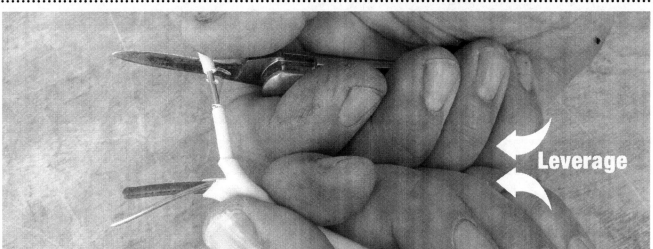

Leverage

WIRE STRIPPERS
007

They can be used for automotive or household electrical. The stripper part is at the back, and the jaws are used for automotive crimp on connectors. Open the handles, put the wire into a hole, squeeze it, and turn the tool to cut the insulation. Pull the insulation off. Use your hand for leverage.

You can also use a knife for the same thing.

EXTERNAL SNAP RING

008 ⟩ SNAP RINGS

There are two kinds, internal and external. You will
need snap ring pliers to install and remove them.
They are adjustable, and will do them both. Found
on lots of machine parts.

Watch here

Not here

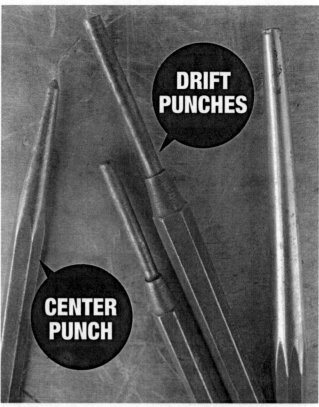

DRIFT PUNCHES

CENTER PUNCH

COLD CHISELS

Keep it straight.

Not whacking your hand is the objective. Focus on the head of the punch, or chisel, when swinging the hammer, not the other end. This is a meditation, with instant Karma, if you loose focus.

IMPORTANT

PALM

HEEL

010 ▷ USING A SCREWDRIVER

A screwdriver should be held so that the "heel" of the hand presses firmly against the end of the handle. This increases the pressure on the notch in the screw, so you minimize the chance of stripping.

If the screw is made in China, apply twice the pressure.

Do not get upset if you still strip the notch. Go get some good quality North American screws, or go to your random parts collection. **Tip 120**.

NEVER use the palm of your hand to apply pressure to a round object like a screwdriver handle. If you do, your hand will hurt for a week after.

Here is the second way to use a screwdriver, with two hands, screwdriver handle pressed into the heel, when the going gets tough, and the cool electric screwdriver you got for Christmas has burned out.

Wear cloth, or light leather gloves for more grip, and to avoid getting blisters.

BASIC
SCREWDRIVERS
YOU SHOULD OWN

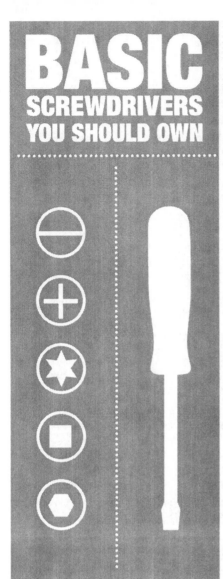

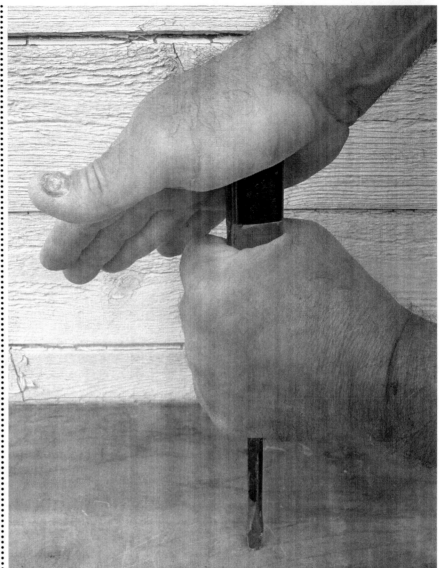

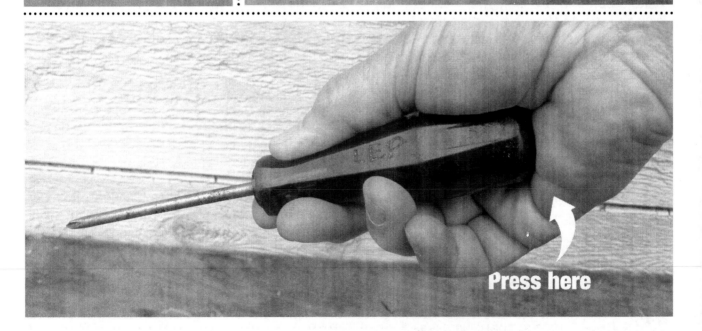

Press here

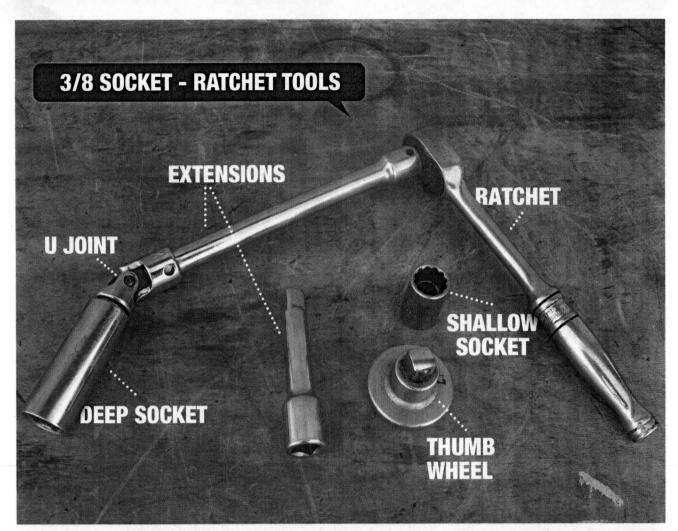

3/8 SOCKET - RATCHET TOOLS

EXTENSIONS

RATCHET

U JOINT

SHALLOW SOCKET

DEEP SOCKET

THUMB WHEEL

011   SOCKETS AND WRENCHES

Sockets come in 3/8 inch, 1/2 inch, and larger sizes. You should also have some extensions, and a ratchet. Other attachments include: a u-joint, and thumb wheel. The thumb wheel goes into the end of a socket, for faster work in tight spots.

Pick the socket or wrench that gives the tightest fit on the head of the nut or bolt. Use, standard (1/2 inch, 9/16 inch, then compare the fit with a metric 12 mm, 13 mm or 14mm socket or wrench).

Deep sockets make it easy to twist a nut with a bolt sticking out of it.

The six point sockets, fit tighter, and are better for bolts and nuts that have worn flats.
The tighter the fit, the lower the chance of rounding the flats on the bolt or nut.

Keep the socket or wrench straight, and tight on the flats when turning. If it slips off, it will damage the flats. Do not over tighten. See: **Tip 68** and **Tip 137**, practice breaking things, and **Tip 114**, tightening things.

This Snap-on ratchet is fast, because it has a fine tooth ratchet inside, and, after the nut is broken loose, the handle acts as a counter weight, while working, if the tool is held in the middle.

The typical wrench is the "combination". It has an "open end," and a "box end." There are many sizes. You should have extras of everything. You can buy good quality wrenches and sockets second hand.

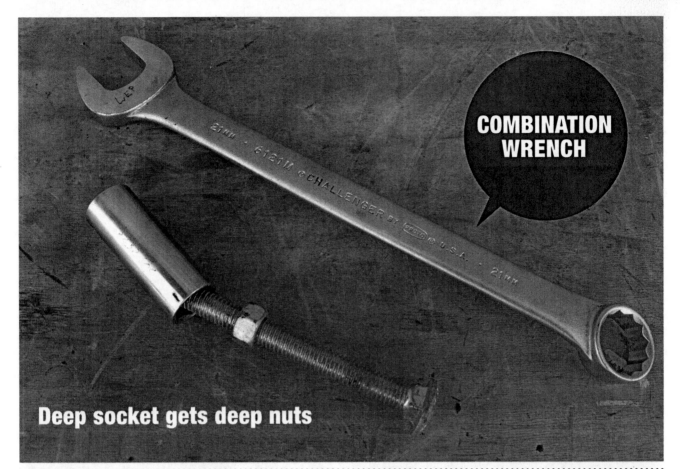

COMBINATION WRENCH

Deep socket gets deep nuts

TWELVE POINT

SIX POINT

ELECTRIC MOTOR

STEEL SHAFT

BRASS BUSHING

ROLLER BEARING

BALL BEARING

012 ▷ BEARINGS AND BUSHINGS

There are two common types of bearings: ball and roller. Roller bearings are used for the most extreme heat and load conditions.

A bushing is usually a metal "sleeve" that a shaft turns on. Usually the bushing is made of softer metal than the shaft. Some can be replaced. Common in small electric motors, both automotive and household. Also found in places where there is a very light "load" on the shaft. Most are replaceable. See: **Tip 108**.

All bearings and bushings need oil or grease. Most are not designed to be easily greased, but you can outsmart the designers. Keep reading.

See: **Tip 95**, oiling bushings. **Tip 125**, greasing bearings.

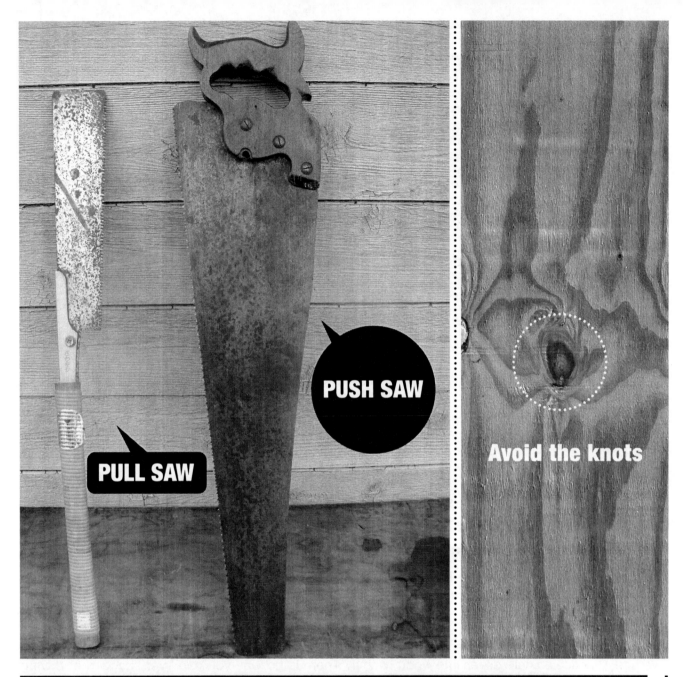

HAND WOOD SAWS

There are two kinds. The kind that you push to cut, and the kind that you pull to cut. The push kind is to be avoided.

Get a Japanese pull saw, you will never go back.

Hold here

▷ **HAMMERS**

The most common metal hammer is the ball peen, but for driving nails, a claw hammer is best. The claws are for pulling bent nails.

Hold a hammer at the end of the handle, to get more leverage. Practice on nails driven into wood, with a claw hammer. Do not practice on galvanized nails, because they bend easily. See if you can drive the nail head right down flush, or level with the board, without denting the wood. Should take four strokes max.

Get "bright" (bare steel) nails. Spit on them if the wood is old and dry. Use WD 40 if there are lots to drive, and you run out of spit.

Practice with the ball peen hammer on some metal. The "ball" end is good for rounding the end of rivets and shaping metal.

If you buy a claw hammer, make sure the face is flat. If you already have one with a domed face, flatten the face with a grinder, and cut groves into the face, with the cutting wheel on your grinder.

There is no way you can ever succeed at driving nails with a hammer that has a face that is domed. It is one of the most poorly designed tools ever made. It will slip off of the head of the nail 90% of the time, damage the wood, and make you feel like it was your fault.

See: **Tip 119**, buying tools.

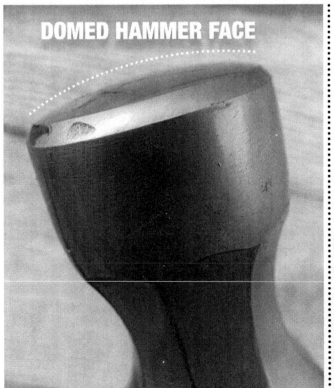

015 ▶ **TIGHTENING AND LOOSENING THINGS**

Clockwise is tighten. Counter clockwise is loosen, except for reverse threads. See: **Tip 69**.

Here is a clock, for all your Digital Age Folks who don't own one of those trendy yet clunky, and very expensive, wrist watches, with a face, and lots of knobs.

016 ▶ **LET YOUR THUMB AND KNUCKLES BE YOUR GUIDE**

We have two thumbs to help repair machines. Use your thumb, or knuckle, as a guide for all sorts of things.

For example, opening a can of paint, getting a drill bit started, placing the tip of a screw driver into a slot.

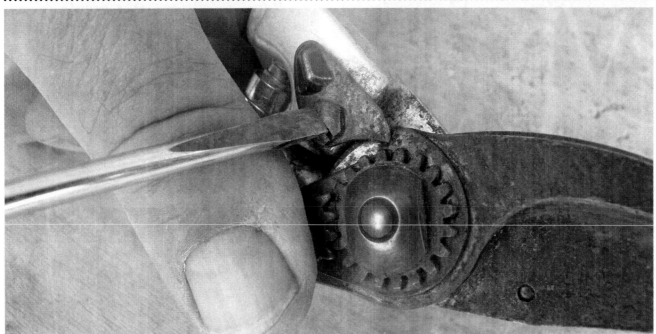

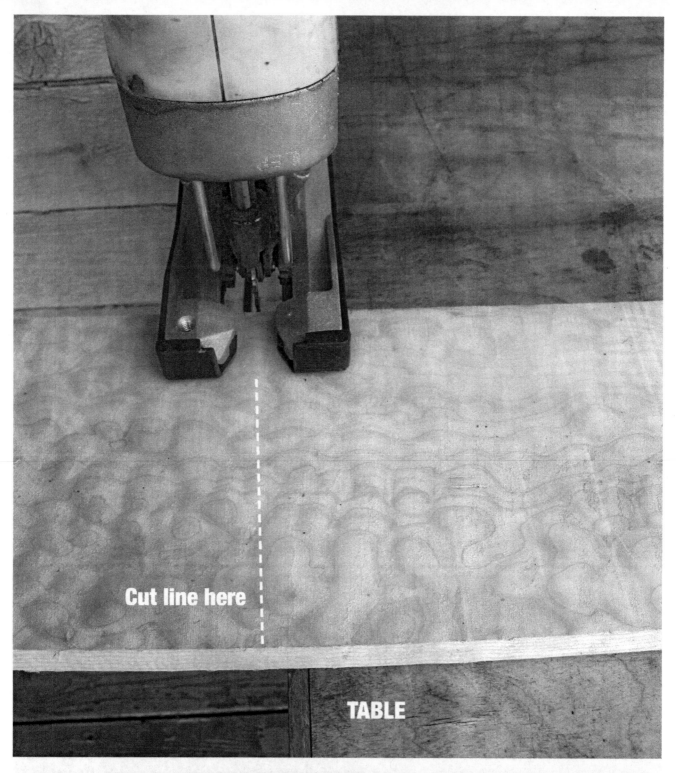

Cut line here

TABLE

TIP 017 — USING AN ELECTRIC JIG SAW

Put the item to be cut on a solid surface, like a
work bench. Do your cutting close to that surface.
It avoids vibrations, and lets you make a cleaner
cut. Especially important with thin metal or wood.

Removing a seal

TIP

Good for seals, and oil filters. See: **Tip 26**, changing oil.

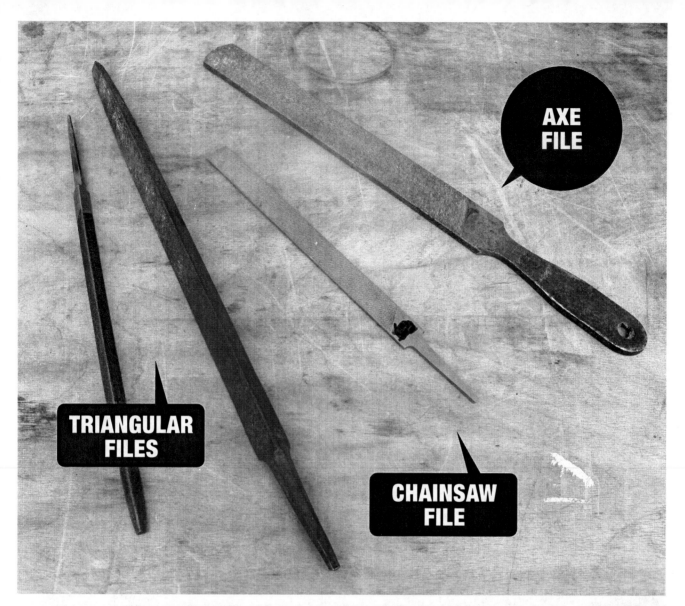

AXE
FILE

TRIANGULAR
FILES

CHAINSAW
FILE

019 ▷ FILES

For metal work, the axe file, flat chainsaw file, and
triangular file are the most important.

020 ▷ TORX

Get a Torx set, lots of appliances are using these.

021 ▷ METRIC AND STANDARD HEX WRENCHES

Make sure you have both, because the world is
complicated

022 ▷ CARDBOARD

Use big pieces on your driveway so you can slip easily under your car. Your clothes will slide on the cardboard before the cardboard slides on the concrete driveway. Now you do not need to buy one of those mechanic's "creepers." Good thing, they have plastic wheels these days, that wear out quickly.

Cardboard catches those messy drops of oil when you remove the oil filter. This is one item that can be disposed of, after use, without feeling guilty.

023 ▷ FOLLOWING THE DIRECTIONS SOMETIMES DOES NOT HELP

In the last five years I have purchased a number of new things. Almost all of them have directions for assembly and/or use which are wrong, or incomplete. So, if you are having trouble putting something together, or using it, call the supplier. Try to shop at places that are local, and have experienced people you can call when something does not work.

One product I bought had such bad directions that I went back to the supplier, who referred me to a You Tube video, produced by the manufacturer. I watched it, and it was wrong as well.

The latest item was a new jet pump, for pumping water out of a well. These things have been around since time began.

This pump was made by a US manufacturer, who got started in 1944. The directions appear to have been printed in the US. There was a glaring error. The plumbing diagram called for a check valve in the wrong place. When assembled, according to the directions, the pump did not work. The check valve prevented the pressure switch from sensing the pressure, so it would not shut off.

The exception seems to be IKEA. They seem to get it right for everything I have purchased from them.

I believe someone could make a great business writing useful and accurate instructions for manufacturers.

024 ▷ BUYING PARTS

This is a very important Basic, so I have included it under each of the three following sections: Automotive, Appliance/Household/Garden, and General.

The most important Basic, however, is to have the old part in your hand when you buy the new one. Compare them carefully.

BRING THE OLD PART WITH YOU *

AUTOMOTIVE

Allegedly , Rudolph Diesel sold one of his new engines to a customer,
but there was trouble making it run. So Herr Diesel visited the customer.
He struck the engine with a hammer. It ran. He then presented his bill
for 150 Marks, a large sum, at the time.

When the customer protested, he said, "Yes, I only hit it with a hammer,
but I knew where to hit it."

THE OIL CAN THAT GOES WITH YOU

TIP

If you forgot your WD 40, and your spray grease,
try the dipstick.

Just put it back clean.

OIL FILTER

PRY BAR

If the oil filter is stuck, it must be removed, or the whole point of the oil change is lost.

Drive the pointed end of a pry bar, or a large screwdriver, through the shell of the filter, and use it for leverage to twist it off. Twist counter clockwise to remove.

Most likely, the metal jacket will tear, if it does not come loose.

If it does tear, try using a hammer and cold chisel, at the base of the filter, nearest the place where it attaches to the engine. Drive the filter base counter clockwise, with the cold chisel, to unscrew.

The reason it was so hard to remove is because an inexperienced person put it on too tight. Change your own oil next time, and it will not happen again.

When installing the new filter, oil the gasket with engine oil, and put it on hand tight. If you have inexperienced hands, use an oil filter tool to tighten NO MORE than one eighth (1/8) turn beyond hand tight.

If you are nervous about the oil leaking out because it was not tight enough, drive it around the block, and crawl underneath, to see if it leaks. I bet it won't.

See "Safety," on page **2** about getting under a car which is on a jack.

Removing the plug. See: **Tip 87**, increase the power of hand tools.

Chances are, the same overly eager person that put your oil filter on too tight, also over tightened the drain plug.

Put it back on with the right amount of torque. See: **Tip 114**, tightening things.

Be sure to take your used oil to a recycler. Places that sell oil, including gas stations often accept used oil.

MY VOLVO

Those are: fuel injector cleaner, methyl hydrate, spray grease, radiator seal ("stop leak") aerosol carburetor cleaner, just to name the major ones. They all have a use, and, in my experience most are worth the money.

Methyl hydrate is available at hardware stores. It is sold at gas stations as "gas line antifreeze." Gasoline often has small amounts of water in it.

By putting a glug or two of methyl hydrate into your full gas tank, you can get rid of the water. Doing this once or twice a year is usually enough.

Aerosol white grease is great for everything that needs to be greased, but is hard to get to, or hard to take apart. Shoot for the place where two surfaces meet. WD 40 is also good. Start with it, if the part is really dry or rusty. Later, use aerosol grease.

Silicone spray. This stuff is cheap. Spray all your rubber stuff, like door seals, to prevent freeze up, and sunroof and trunk seals to prevent leaks. Also works in locks to prevent freeze up, but WD 40 is better in locks.

Oil additives, like "motor honey", are good for a really worn engine, the ones that burn more than one quart in 300 to 500 miles. It will slow the oil burning, and make it quieter. Johnsen's, and STP are two good brands.

These products are the consistency of honey, hence the name. You have nothing to loose, because the engine is almost finished anyway.

TEST LIGHT

ALLIGATOR CLIP

028 ▷ HOW TO FIND WHERE AUTO ELECTRICAL PROBLEMS ARE

Always look for the most obvious thing first. Like a blown fuse, or a loose or dirty wire.

Use a test light for auto electrical to see what's hot, and what's not. The pointed tip can be pushed right through the insulation, without damage, so you can see if a wire has power.

See: **Tip 36**, auto electrical problems.

Before you start, test the light by connecting one end to the positive and one end to the negative poles on the battery.

Usually, the power, or hot wire is red, and the ground wire is black. Remember that some red wires will only be hot when the key is turned on.

DO NOT use a test light on household electrical wires. There are other testers for household electrical problems.

Auto electrical systems are complicated these days, so do not get discouraged if you cannot figure it out. It might be a relay, not wiring.

There are books published for many kinds of cars that have wiring diagrams. Find them at your public library.

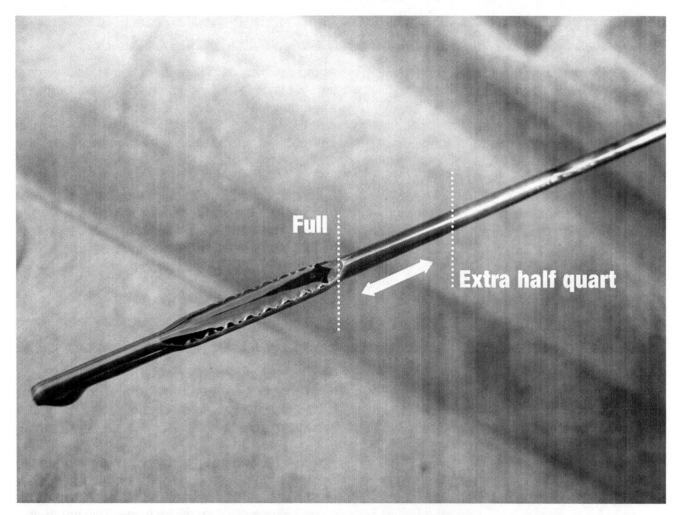

Full

Extra half quart

PERSUADE YOUR ENGINE TO LAST LONGER

Keep engine oil about 1/2 liter (1/2 quart) above dip stick "full" line.

Every engine burns oil, so if you just fill the crankcase to the "full" line, on the dipstick, you will be low in a day or two.

The reason the level of oil matters is because there are two kinds of lubrication going on inside the engine. Pressurized oil to bearings, (the red light on the dash) and "splash" oiling for everything else. Some cars have a "low oil" light too.

Outsmart your engine, and put in a bit more oil. It will not harm the engine, and, in my experience, will make it last longer, and give you better gas mileage. There is more oil to splash around, to lubricate and cool parts.

This is one place where I disagree with my Volvo Owner's Manual. It says that the engine will burn more oil if the oil level is high. That is not my experience in driving my last 3 Volvos over 1,000,000 miles total.

I prefer heavier oil in the summer, 20/50, because it gives more protection. In the winter, if you live where it is cold, use 10/30. In the spring you can add 20/50 to the 10/30 until you change oil.

Check the engine oil level in the morning, before the car is driven. If you have a car that you know burns a lot of oil, pick one day per week, and religiously check it on that day. Maybe on Sunday morning. If it is a really old oil burner, say a small prayer each Sunday when you check the oil.

Friction is the machine's second worst enemy. Dirt is the first. Use clean grease.

Grease is the cure-all for a vast number of problems. 2 cents worth of grease can save hundreds of dollars to replace burned out parts. When something is squeaking or running slow, take it apart and grease it.

Use regular automotive grease, or aerosol white grease for hard to reach places.

Battery cables, light plug-ins, and almost everything electrical needs grease. Especially in those cold, salted road zones. There is friction in your electrical system. It is those electrons zipping through the wires that makes the connections dirty.

The road salt acts as catalyst for corrosion, especially on electrical stuff.

Auto electricity flows through the frame of the car (ground). Grease those places where a wire is bolted to the frame. This is especially good for yellow headlights. "Frame" includes any metal part bolted to the metal body of the car.

Car electrical systems are usually 12 volt direct current. That means that there are "hot" wires, usually red, and "ground" wires, usually black, or brown. Car electrical motors, lights, etc. will not work unless grounded to the frame of the car, with a clean connection .

See: **Tip 36**, electrical problems.

With the exception of the spark coil, automotive electrical will not hurt you. Holding a spark plug wire with the engine running will give you a big jolt, with no lasting damage, unless you have a pacemaker.

When you ask a friend for a jump start for your car, hook up the jumper cables to your battery, but make sure the other end is safe, so they cannot short out. See picture. Your friend should leave the engine running for a few minutes after you hook up your battery. Then try to start your car, with the friend's engine still running.

You can grab a hot wire, and touch the frame of the car, you will not feel a thing, unless you are really sensitive. However, if you touch that hot wire to the frame, without a light or motor in between, you will get sparks and heat. The bigger the wire, the more sparks and heat.

Take the negative battery cable off first. The reason is so that when you remove the positive, or hot battery cable it cannot short to ground through the wrench you are using.

When recharging a battery that has removable caps, hydrogen gas is produced. In a confined space, enough can accumulate to cause a mini explosion when exposed to a spark, or flame. This happened to me once, on a minus 20 day, up in the Rockies. It blew out the end of the battery.

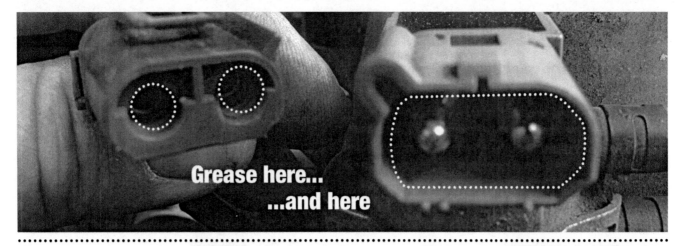

Grease here...
...and here

Never have rings on your fingers, while working on machines.

I once had a gold ring on when working with a battery. I did not follow **Tip 31**. I failed to remove the negative battery terminal first. When I was trying to remove the positive battery terminal, with a wrench, the ring shorted between the wrench in my hand, which was on the positive terminal and ground, and got red hot. The scar on my finger is still there.

Also, when using a wrench, the ring can injure your hand and finger.

TIP  **033** DON'T LOSE HARDWARE

Much time is wasted looking for a nut on the ground. Hubcaps, when cars still had them, were great for lug nuts. When disassembling something, have more than one container for the various layers of the machine.

See: **Tip 110**, take it apart so you can put it back together again.

PARTS

Additionné de vitamines A et D

1 L

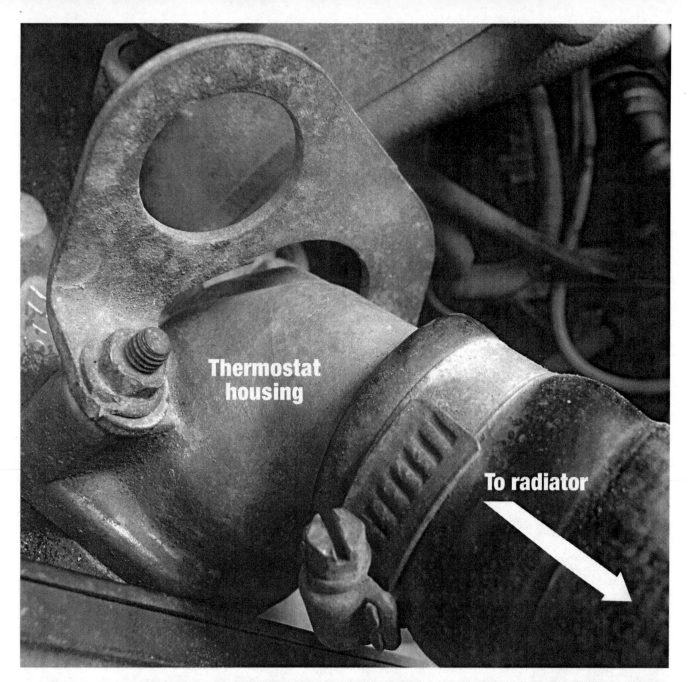

Thermostat housing

To radiator

| 034 | AUTO THERMOSTAT |

Engine temperature gauge looks a little low. Poor gas mileage. Replace with a 190 degree F thermostat. You could put a vitamin C tablet under the flap, so there will be no air pockets. It will dissolve, and make your engine better able to fight off colds.

Engine runs too hot, see: **Tip52**.

EASY REMOVAL OF STUCK RUBBER HOSES

Stick the blade of a large screw driver between the hose end, and the pipe it is stuck to. If it is a small hose, like a vacuum hose, use the procedure in **Tip 85**.

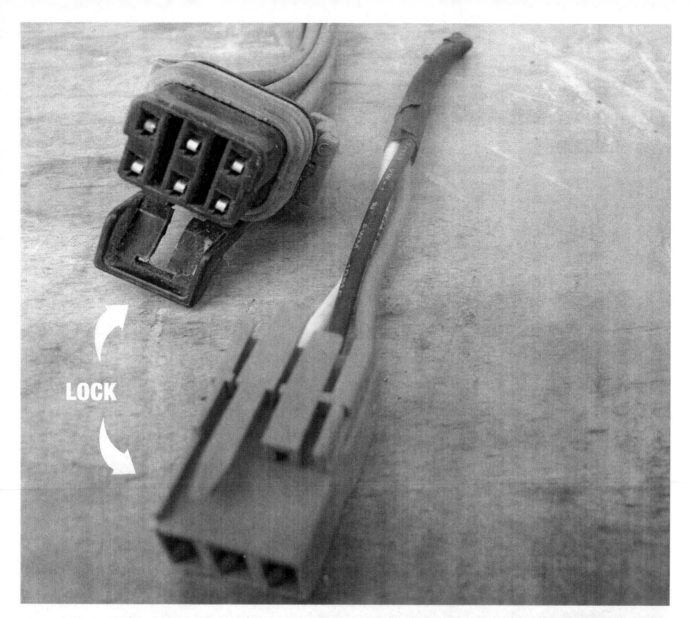

LOCK

036 ▷ AUTO ELECTRICAL PROBLEMS

You will find dirt, broken wires, or poor connections 90% of the time. Look for the obvious.

Pull electrical plug-ins apart, and push them back together several times to restore the connection, then grease them. Usually there is a plastic lock you must squeeze.

Auto electricity flows through the frame of the car (ground) There must be a clean connection wherever a ground wire attaches to the frame. "Frame" includes any metal part of the car that is connected to the frame.

Use the test light with the alligator clip on the positive battery terminal. Poke around with the pointed end to find a good ground.

To fix a bad ground, sand the connection, grease it, and screw it down tight.

See: **Tip 28**, finding auto electrical problems.

HOW TO MAKE A CAR BATTERY POST BIGGER　　　　037

Use a chisel to score the sides of the post, all around. The chisel will make grooves in the soft lead, making the post larger in diameter. Grease it, when you put the cable back on. There must be a tight, clean connection at both poles of the battery, or trouble starting may result.

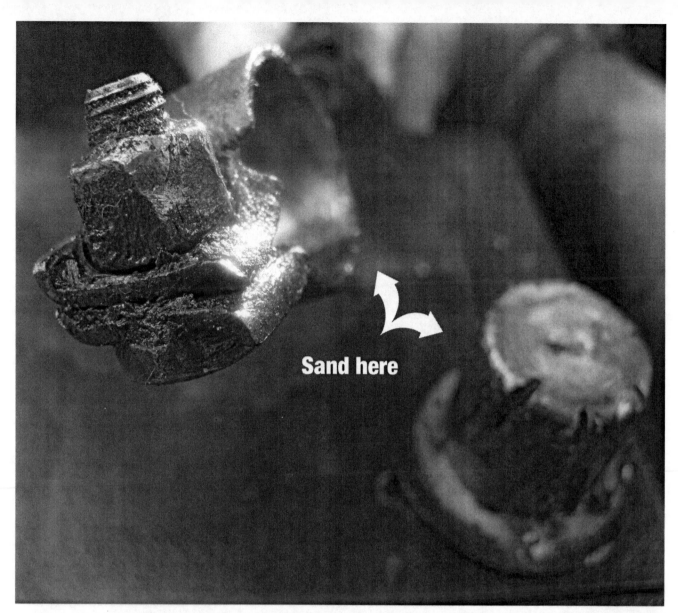

Sand here

038   TROUBLE GETTING YOUR STARTER TO CRANK THE ENGINE

The number one problem, especially in the summer, is loose or corroded battery terminals. Take the cable off, use sand paper, or a battery terminal wire brush, to scrape the inside of the terminal and the outside of the post on the battery. This will remove the corrosion. Sand lightly, until the metal is shiny.

You cannot see the corrosion that has built up, but it will slow the recharging to the point of no recharging. Do not replace any charging system components, like the alternator or regulator, or battery, until you have tried this trick, and run the engine to see if it recharges.

The little red light on the dash will not come on if you have this problem. Your battery will just go dead. I really do not know why they put those lights on the dash. Maybe it is just to tell you when the engine is not running. Like you needed help on that one.

Acid can collect in a dry form on the side of a battery. Keep the battery away from your clothes.

Grease the terminal connections when re-assembling.

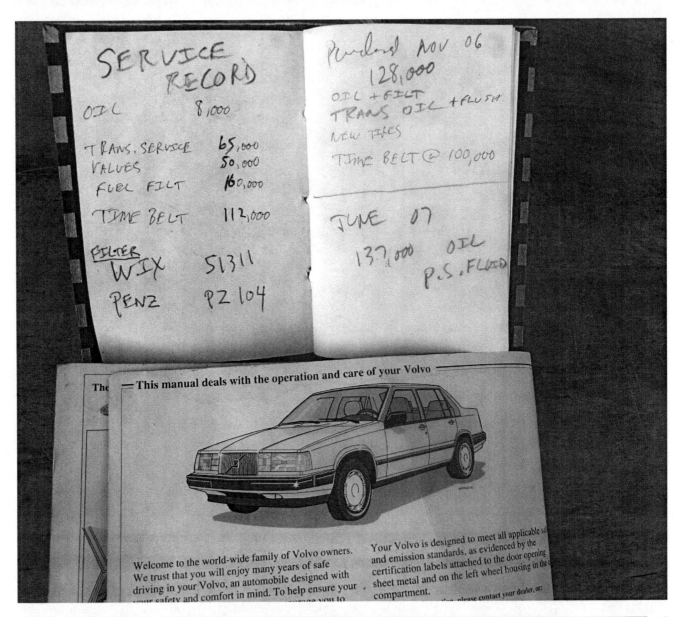

The manufacturer will give you important information about your machine. How it goes together, and comes apart, but most importantly, how to care for it.

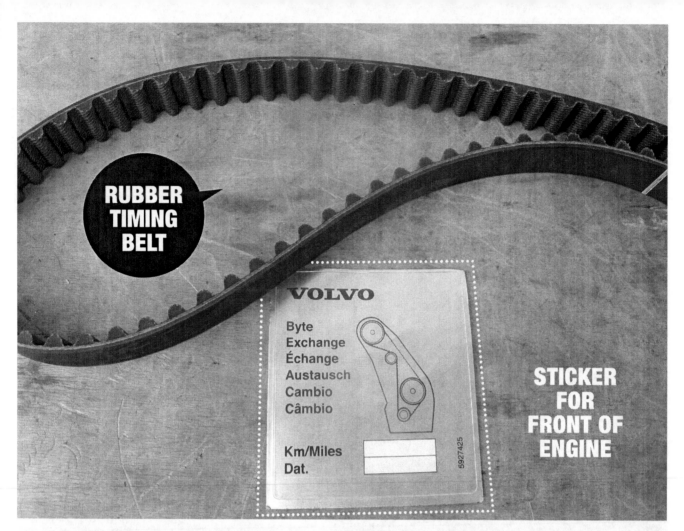

RUBBER TIMING BELT

VOLVO

Byte
Exchange
Échange
Austausch
Cambio
Câmbio

Km/Miles
Dat.

5927425

STICKER FOR FRONT OF ENGINE

TIP 040 ▶ MAKE A SERVICE RECORD

Most owners manuals have a service schedule, for things like changing the oil, checking the tire pressure, etc. Get a little notebook, and keep track of when you did the required service. Stick to the schedule.

Believe it or not, the manufacturers of cars, and other machines, actually tell you how to make them last longer, but I bet 80% of us never read the manual. Servicing your car on schedule is VERY IMPORTANT.

TIP 041 ▶ RUBBER TIMING BELTS AND ARMAGEDDON

There is more than one make of car out there that has a replaceable rubber timing belt on the engine. Some of these cars have "special" engines. The belt must be replaced at precise intervals. If it breaks, your engine will SELF DESTRUCT. No kidding ! This type of engine is called an "interference engine." Google it to see if you own one of these lemons.

Some "aftermarket" (that is, not made by the manufacturer) timing belts are engineered by the same guys who make batteries fail exactly three months after the pro-rated warranty expires. See: **Tip 46**.

GO RENT A TORQUE WRENCH FOR THE DAY 042 TIP

Most complicated machines, like cars, have published torque values for each nut and bolt. They may be expressed in Nm (Newton meters) Or Ft/lb, or Lb/ft, which is short for foot/pounds. I am not sure what a "Newton" is, but a foot pound, is one pound of pressure on a one foot bar, or the equivalent.

Either way, it is a guide. 10 foot pounds extra will not destroy anything, but on some things 10 foot pounds too little may, in time, cause problems.

Equipment rental places have torque wrenches you can rent, and practice with. Try a new clean nut and bolt. Tighten to 30 foot pounds, and see how much effort it takes to get loose. Then tighten the same nut by hand, and use the torque wrench to take it loose. See how many foot pounds it takes to get it loose.

See: **Tip 114**, tightening things.

THE VISIT TO THE "FULL SERVE" GAS STATION 043 TIP

Never let a gas station jockey touch your car, except to fill it with gas.

There are not many full service stations anymore, but if you run across one, keep in mind that the

day before this person started pumping gas they were likely unemployed, and know nothing about machinery.

THE VISIT TO THE TIRE SHOP 044 TIP

Never let a tire guy put your wheel back on with an impact gun. OK to remove with one. Confirm with the front counter guy that they will use a torque wrench to tighten the lug nuts.

If an impact gun is used to put the wheel back on, chances are it will be severely over tightened, and when you have a flat, on a dark and stormy night, that crummy little tire tool they gave you with the car

will be useless. The wheel bolts, or lug bolts should be just tight enough that your manufacturer supplied wrench will take them loose.

Gap is three
times too big

045 SPARK PLUGS AND GETTING TO WORK ON TIME

Plugs are supposed to be replaced every 35,000 miles (50,000 km) or so. Read the manual, and your Service Record. If your car turns over briskly, but does not start, your job may be on the line.

The main reason for hard starting (when the engine turns over properly), is worn spark plugs. The other is no gasoline getting to the spark plug. A worn plug looks like this.

If you experience hard starting, and do not want to spend the money on new plugs, take them out, and re-gap them.

Don't pull on the wires. Pull on the boot at the end of the wire. Use a special socket (usually 13/16 inch) with a rubber insert. The rubber insert helps you avoid breaking the ceramic upper part of the plug. Hold the socket straight when taking it out, or putting it in.

While the plug is out, just after trying to start the car, see if it looks "wet" and smells of gasoline.

See: **Tip 82**, use your nose.

You can squeeze the top electrode closer to the middle electrode to improve the spark and make starting easier.

If you have a spark plug gap tool (cheap at an auto parts place), set the gap at .025 of an inch.

If you don't have a gap tool, put a butter knife in between the two electrodes, and tap the moveable outer one, with a hammer, to tighten the gap.

Replace the plugs before winter. When you put the new plug in, it needs a little extra tightening to compress the new gasket.

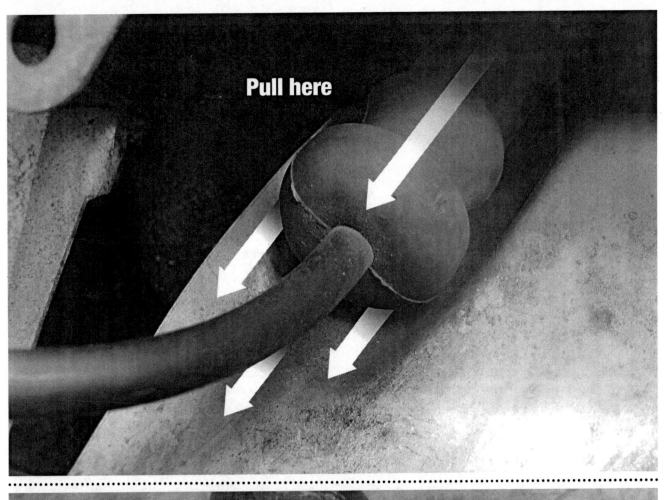

Pull here

Use a butter knife to set the gap

It usually happens just after the pro-rated warranty expires. If you are going into winter with 4.5 years on a 5 year battery, replace it before you get stuck. The battery will answer its Master's Call, and quit in a heart beat, at 5 years and 3 months.

I have often wondered how engineers can be so precise in making things fail.

There are usually stick-ons with punched holes on the battery that indicate its age.

Spray belt conditioner
on inside of belt

BELT DRESSING AND BELT ADJUSTMENT

If your car makes that embarrassing squealing sound, when you turn the wheel, or step on the gas, it is probably because a belt is loose. A belt adjustment on a car takes about 15 minutes. Look it up on the net, or ask someone how to do it. It is really simple.

But, if you are in a hurry, buy a can of Permatex belt dressing, and spray it on the moving belt. Watch those fingers. This will buy you a few days.

Keep in mind that the belt wears much faster when it has been squealing, and will need replacement soon.

See: **Tip 39**, read the manual.

Some car manufacturers will tell you about this, some will not. You cannot go wrong replacing this stuff now and then, perhaps every other year. Fluids get hot, then pick up dirt, water, and pieces of the machine. Dirt is a machine's worst enemy.

The fluid is really, really cheap compared to the cost of the parts they flow through.

Take the cap off of the master cylinder, if the fluid inside is not clear, change it.

To replace the brake fluid, open the bleeder nipples on the back and front wheels. Use a box end wrench. Pump the brake pedal, while refilling the master cylinder with brake fluid. Have a bleeder bottle on each open nipple.

Make a bleeder bottle with a clear pop bottle, and short piece of rubber hose that will grip the bleeder nipple. The hose should go all the way to the bottom of the bottle. This will collect the used fluid, and let you see when the new clean fluid is coming through.

Some cars have anti-lock brakes. This makes the job more complicated. Get some instructions for your particular car.

Most cars have power brakes. The engine does not need to be running during this procedure.

CAREFULLY road test the car to make sure you did not get any air into the lines. (My lawyer says to tell you to leave this whole thing to the professionals. By doing it wrong, you might cause serious personal injury, and/or wreck your car).

If you did get air in the system, do it all over again. If you got air in the lines, it was because you let the fluid level in the master cylinder reservoir fall too low while pumping the brakes, and you pumped in some air.

Air will make the pedal feel "soft". The brakes may "fade" during hard braking. Look this one up on the net. There is lots of good advice there.

To replace the power steering fluid, start by disconnecting the return line. Start the engine and run for a FEW SECONDS. Catch the oil in a container, as it comes out. Replace with new fluid. Do not run the pump dry.

This is often an instant cure for pump noise and/or a "jerky", or hard to turn steering wheel.

If the fluid smells burned, replace it twice, with a short drive in between.

BLEEDER NIPPLE

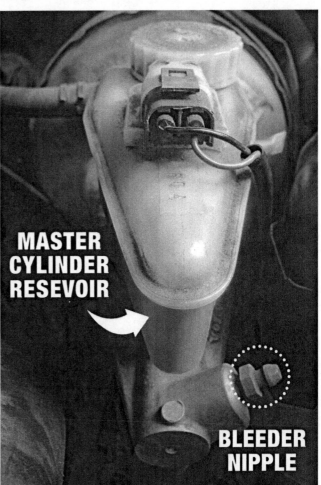

MASTER CYLINDER RESEVOIR

BLEEDER NIPPLE

RETURN LINE

USE APPROVED POWER STEERING FLUID ONLY

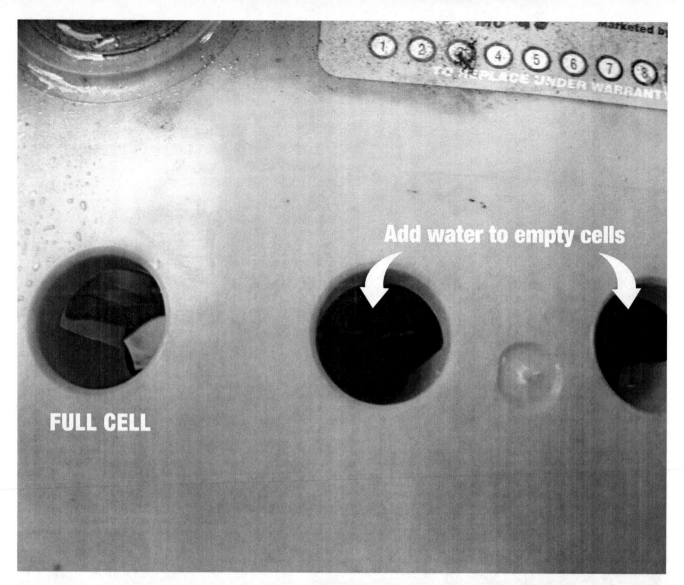

Add water to empty cells

FULL CELL

GETTING STARTED IN MINNESOTA IN JANUARY

Take your battery into the house on very cold nights, or trickle charge.

Most modern batteries have handles, and are sealed, so the chance of contact with acid is reduced.

A warm battery will start your car way better than a cold one.

If your battery has removable caps for filling with water, make sure the water level is up to the "split ring," or to the point where it is about 1/2 inch from the top of the hole. Also make sure you do not get any of the battery contents on your clothes, or they will look like "Designer" clothes with holes.

Use distilled water. "Hard water" will leave deposits and cause your batery to fail even sooner.

See **Tip 46**, batteries are designed to fail.

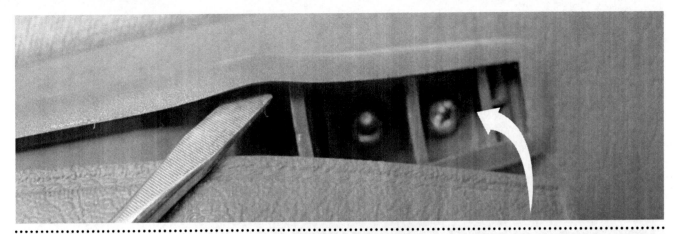

Snap out plastic cover hidden screws inside

Dashboard plastic snaps out

Getting beyond the plastic housings on many parts of cars is a big part of the repair. Visit an auto re-cycler. They have lots of cars in various states of disassembly. You can find your make and model, and take a look. The year does not matter much, because, the fasteners stay mostly the same for several years running.

If they will let you wander around in the yard, and most will, take a few tools, and practice on their cars, before you tackle your own.

Here are two ways these things work.

See: **Tip 110**, take it apart so you can put it back together again.

See: **Tip 111**, put hardware in containers

Dirt is a machine's worst enemy. Friction and heat are the next worst.

If you open your car engine, for example to adjust valves, or replace a metal timing chain, change the oil after, because dirt always gets in. When re-packing bearings, make sure they are clean before the grease goes in.

Clean everything in solvent, with a stiff parts brush. Blow dry with compressed air. If you do not have compressed air, use a rag to dry it, shake it, and/ or let it air dry for a day. If the part needs oil inside, lightly oil it before re-assembly

Turn cap 1/4 to loosen

Before you mess with the thermostat (**Tip34**) make sure you have a 50/50 antifreeze water mix in the cooling system, (**Tip 39**, read the manual) Even if you live where freezing temperatures only occur in an ice maker, you should run this mix. Antifreeze is also a summer coolant. It does not boil, except in Saudi Arabia, or in Space.

If you have a leak, in the radiator, or hoses, do these two things. 1. Buy a tube of "Stop Leak", which is some sort of black granules that plug leaks, and put it into the radiator. 2. Loosen the radiator cap so that it does not build up pressure.

The idea with pressurizing a cooling system is to raise the boiling point of water, but since you are not using pure water it does not matter, in an emergency.

053 ▷ PUTTING IT BACK TOGETHER AGAIN

When trying to assemble something, especially in tight quarters, holding the parts together with Vice Grips makes it easier to put in the bolt, and proper washer pile up before putting on the nut.

If there are several bolts that have to be put in, you can also do a "preliminary assembly" with only the bolt and nut. Now you can bring the two parts together, put in more bolts, with proper washer pile ups, and a nut, then go back and add the washers to the first one.

See: **Tip 105**, use a punch to align parts.

See: **Tip 107**, washer pile ups.

Rebuilding an engine is complicated. If you get as far as the crankshaft, and other internal moving parts,

put some grease on new bearings and seals when re-assembling. Oil the pistons and rings. This will give the parts some protection on start up, if the oil pump does not deliver promptly.

On first start after rebuilding, add new oil, and disconnect the power wire to the coil. Turn the engine over with the starter, with the spark plugs removed. Keep doing it until the oil light goes out. That means you have oil pressure. Put the plugs back in, and the wire back on, and fire it up.

See: **Tip 110**, take it apart, so you can put it back together again.

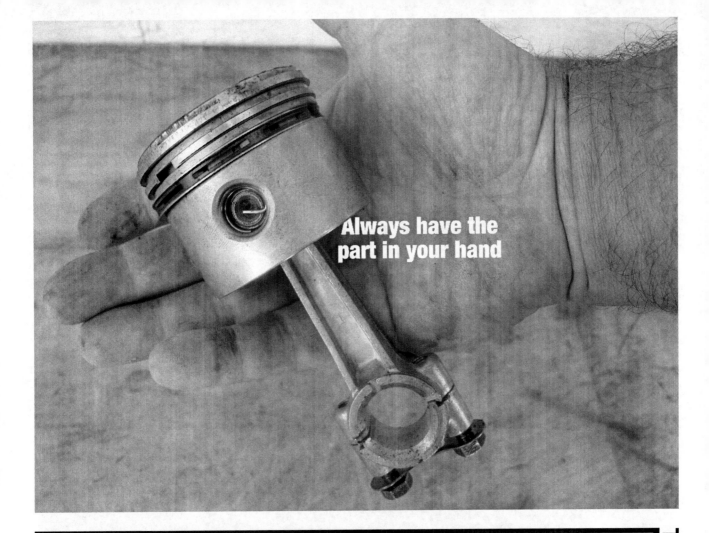
Always have the part in your hand

BUYING PARTS

Replacement items, like spark plugs, oil, oil and air filters, brake pads and hoses are cheapest at an auto parts store. They have books that can cross reference your make and model with all "aftermarket" parts.

Most components are cheapest at auto recyclers (junk yards). I have bought many parts at these places, and they are a real bargain. I am always amazed at how low the mileage is on most wrecked cars. Almost all have mileage under 80,000 miles, or 125,000 kilometers.

Just about any part of your car can be found at an auto recycler.

Cost is usually one half of new, on large items. However, on older cars you can get them even cheaper.

Sometimes you have to remove the parts yourself, but that should make them even cheaper.

Have the old part in your hand when you visit the auto recycler. Compare carefully.

As a last resort, you may have to go to the Dealership. They are the most expensive.

APPLIANCE
HOUSEHOLD
GARDEN

There is an old, and true expression:
" The woman who cuts her own wood is warmed twice by it."

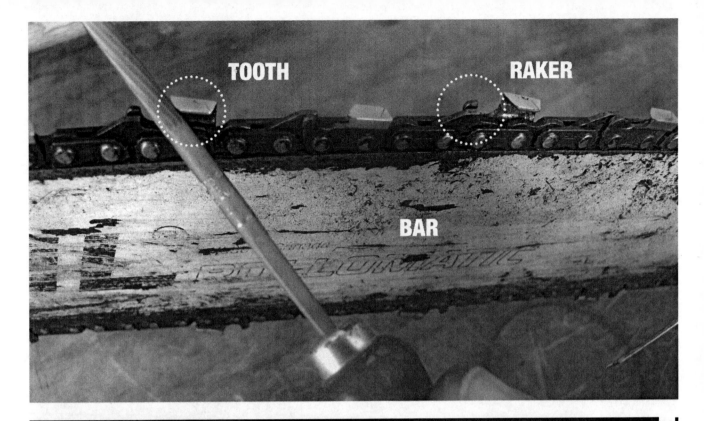

TOOTH RAKER BAR

Read the manual. Keep the chain sharp and tight.

Cut some wood, and get a modern wood stove, (the kind with air injection in the smoke path), and enjoy friendly heat.

Every city is full of free wood. Pallets, dead trees, and construction waste. BUT watch out for treated lumber. Normally it is a sickly green color, or it is a putrid brown. NEVER burn this stuff anywhere. It is toxic.

If you live near the ocean, do not burn drift wood. The salt in the wood will eat up your stove. Get some advice from the stove salesperson, or buy a book about cleaning your chimney, and other safety issues.

Sharpening the chain is a real art form. Use the manu-facturer's suggested round file. Try to match the angle of the tooth. Try the file on the chain before you wear it out, so you know what the angle of the tooth looks like.

File the links on one side, say 3 strokes each. Then, turn the saw around, and do the other side, same number of strokes. Use pressure on the forward stroke, none on the return stroke.

If one side has shorter links, because you filed it more

than the other side, the saw will cut crooked.
You can cut the rakers, or depth gauge with a flat chain saw file, or an electric grinder.

The grinder is much faster and better. Flat files are made for the woodcutter in the bush, but you probably keep your chain saw close to an electrical outlet. Save the flat file for your blender.

The lower the rakers are, the bigger the chunk of wood is cut out. For soft wood, big chunks mean fast cutting. With hard wood, the saw will buck a bit, like a bronco, if the chunks are too big. Just go slower.

Do not run the saw full throttle. Instead, run it at the speed where you get the best cutting.

All chain saw engines are "two stroke". They must have special oil mixed with the gas. Buy a separate gas can for the mixed oil and gas. It is helpful to get a can that holds the right amount of gas for one bottle of saw oil. Write "SAW" on it, because if you (or one of your kids) accidentally pours mixed gas into your lawnmower, it will foul the spark plug, and the combustion chamber.

Wear safety glasses, chain jamming pants, gloves, steel toed boots, and ear plugs, my lawyer says to tell you.

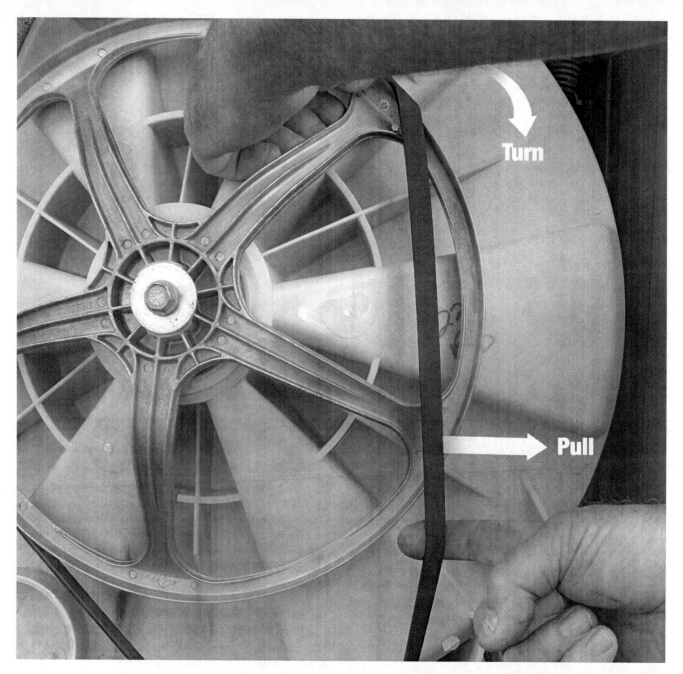

Turn

Pull

056 ▷ PUTTING RUBBER BELTS BACK ON

Get the belt onto one pulley. Slowly rotate the
other pulley while forcing the belt over the edge.
Be careful, it will bite you.

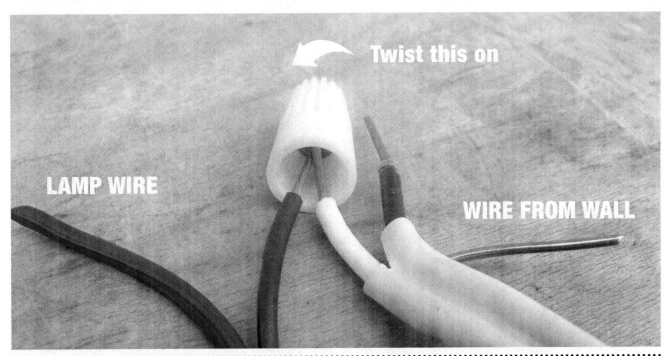

Attach two or three wires without tape, or solder. Start with the wires straight, twist on a wire nut, or Marette. This device will twist the wires together, hold them, and insulate them, all at once. It can be used for solid copper, strand lamp wire, or automotive wires.

I do not recommend using a wire nut in an auto electrical system, unless it is wrapped in electrical tape too. The vibrations will dislodge it eventually.

They can also be used for attaching lamp wire to solid copper. Light fixtures are usually lamp wire, either copper or steel, and attach to solid copper wires that come out of the wall.

Spit goes here

Be sure to put the gasket in

Duct tape prevents cuts from the clamp

058 REPAIR A GARDEN HOSE

Garden hoses come in 1/2 inch, 5/8 inch and 3/4 inch. Buy a replacement fitting and hose clamps. Cut off the old piece, and install the new one. Use a little spit. Duct tape the hose clamp, or it will cut you every time you use the hose.

See **Tip136**, Spit and bailing wire.

Hose clamps are good for fixing all sorts of things. Any round thing that needs support can benefit from one. Like the head of a broom where the handle screws in. If it is weak, add a hose clamp.

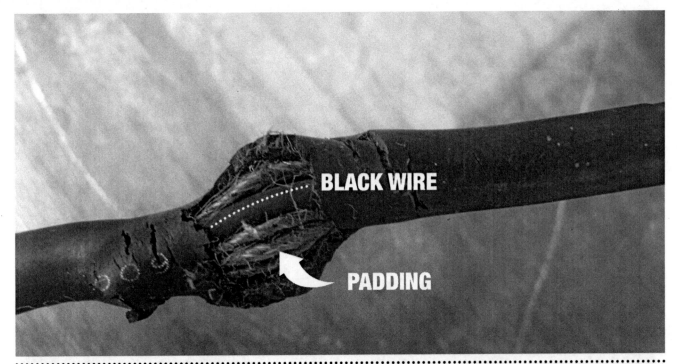

BLACK WIRE

PADDING

Tape over this end

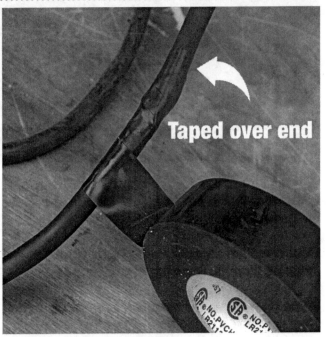

Taped over end

Good for repairing electrical cords, or insulating a newly repaired wire.

Unplug the appliance, and look at the white and black wires inside, where the outer covering is frayed. If the black and/or white wires have frayed insulation, they should be individually taped, before you tape the outer covering.

Start the tape so that the first end is wrapped up. That leaves only one loose end.

Grease the derailleur

TIP | 060 ▷ BICYCLES

Use spray grease on the chain, derailleur, and sprockets. Get a pro to adjust the spokes if the rim goes wiggly.

Most bikes are cheaply made, so be careful about stripping threads, rounding bolts and nuts.

Some bikes have left hand threads on one pedal. They are usually marked.

After it sits out all winter, you will need lots of WD 40 to get stuck parts moving.

Write down the serial number, so when it gets stolen, you have a small chance of getting it back. I got a bike back this way, and that was in the early 80's when there were not many computers.

There is now a National Bike Registry, and a Stolen Bike Registry. Google them.

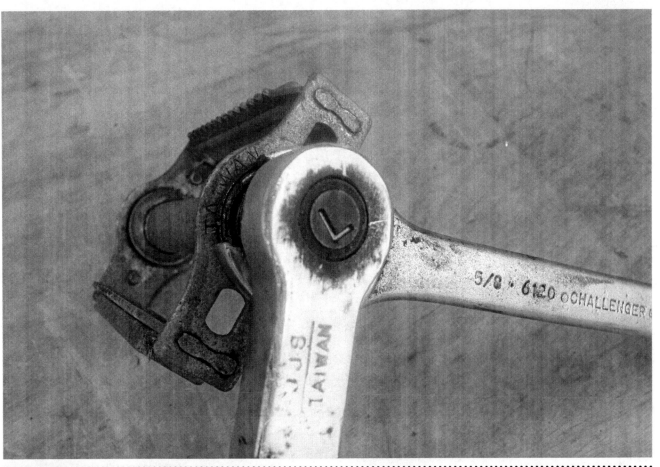

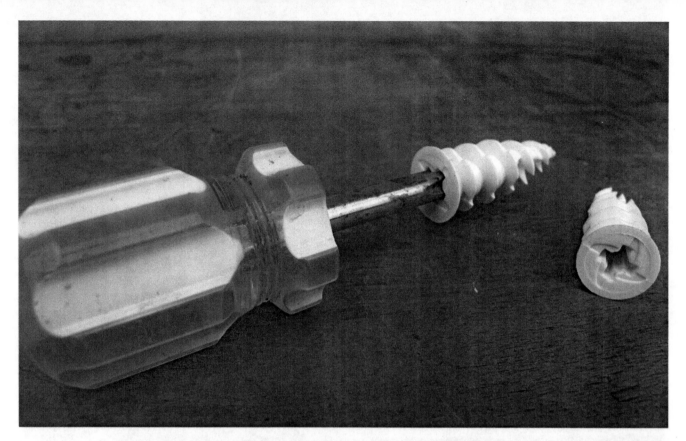

TIP 061 ▸ WALL ANCHORS

One kind is better than most of the others. Here it is.

Drill the right size hole in your gyproc wall, and screw it in. Then you can put a screw into the anchor for hanging pictures, or installing towel racks. Make sure the screw you use in the anchor is the right size.

TIP 062 ▸ CLEAN UP THAT STEAM IRON THAT YOU MELTED STUFF ON

Use steel wool.

TIP 063 ▸ SHARPENING SCISSORS

Use a flat chain saw file, rub it along each blade. Press only on the forward stroke. Then, if it has a rivet, instead of a screw, tighten the rivet, with a ball peen hammer. Use the anvil at the back of a vise to work on.

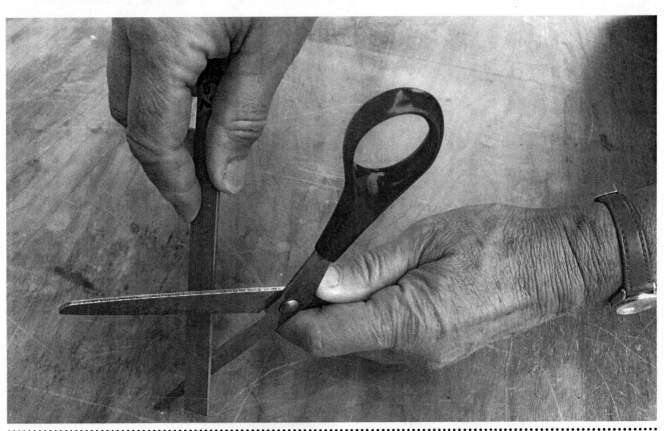

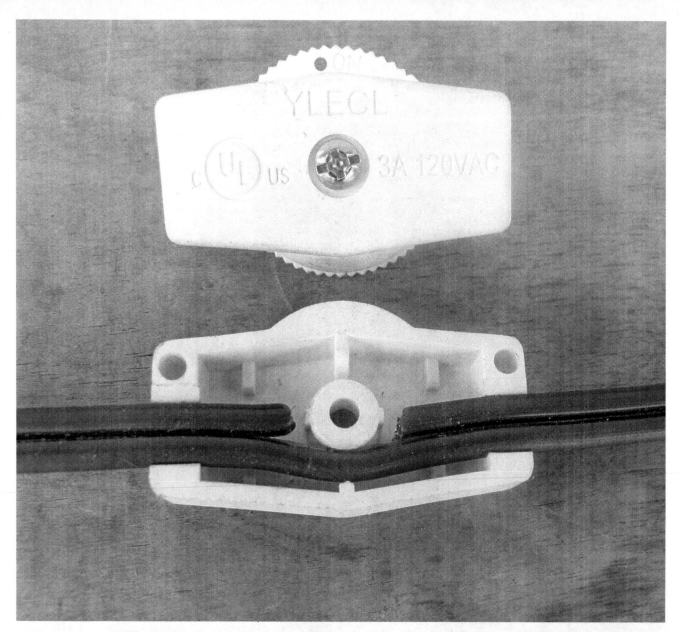

064 ▷ OUTSMART CHEAP CHINESE MADE LAMPS

The little knob that turns the bulb on will fail in three or four years, and it cannot be fixed. So outsmart the manufacturer. Go buy an inline switch, at the hardware store. Attach it to the cord, before the switch fails.

Install it about 12 inches from the base of the lamp. Follow the directions on the package. Anyone can do it.

Leave the original switch "on" and use the new in-line switch to switch the lamp off and on.

Most makers of "lamp wire" put a little ridge on one wire. Lamp wire is light weight electrical wire for, of all things, lamps.

The ridge on one wire helps you tell which is which after a few feet, incase you want to use it for speaker wire. It is also there to help you attach the black wire coming out of the wall, to the proper prong on the plug, or receptacle.

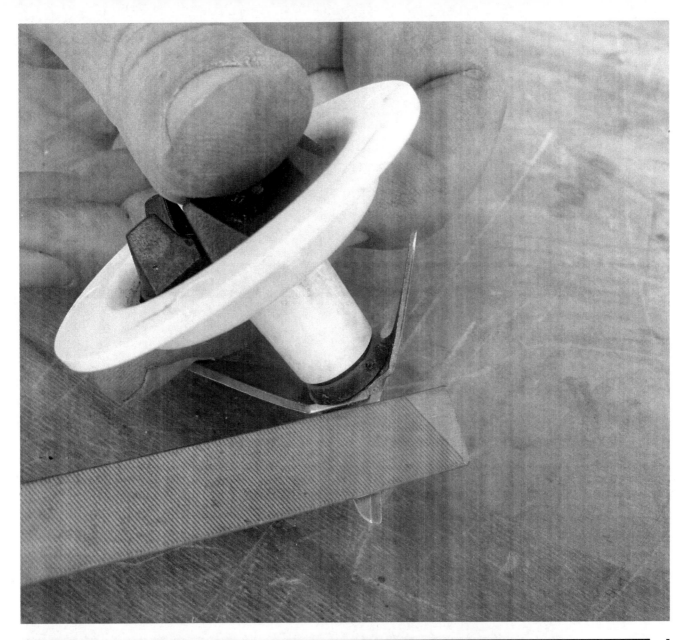

SHARPENING BLENDER BLADES

Get a small metal file. A flat Oregon chain saw file is good. File the cutting surface of each blade. Get out the Tequilla.

TIP 066 ▷ SHARPENING LAWN MOWER BLADES

Remove the blade. Often they are rusty, and the bolt is stuck.

See **Tip 87**, increase power of hand tools.

Use the blade for leverage, remember metal things will hurt you.

Use a grinder to restore the cutting edge. This is not a precision job.

TIP 067 ▷ OIL THAT SEWING MACHINE

The owner's manual should have a map of places to oil, both on top, and underneath.

Use light oil, 10 or 20 weight engine oil, or sewing machine oil.

Put a drop or two into every place where two metal parts rub, and/or where the manual says to put it.

TIP 068 ▷ PRACTICE BREAKING THINGS

The only way you will get to know how much force to apply when turning or hitting things, is to practice, by applying too much force.

So, get a 3/8 bolt, for starters, and put a nut on it, put it in a vise. Twist the nut until it strips.

Whack a grade 2 bolt, then a grade 5 bolt, with a ball peen hammer to see the damage. See **Tip 102**, about hardware grades.

When a difficult problem arises, set up a test on a similar part.

Let your destructive instincts run wild with spare parts. Then you will know how far you can go.

Get a junked appliance, and take it apart. The more things you take apart, the more you will know about fixing your appliance when it fails. Save the screws, nuts and bolts for your random parts collection.

Unscrew counter clockwise, and tighten clockwise. Give it some thought when on your back looking up at something.

The only exception to this is that rare machine, such as my Stihl weed whacker, some bicycles, and some cars made up to about 1970. Reverse threads were found on the right side of the wheels on the car. The weed whacker head on the Stihl has reverse threads.

Most of these things will be marked, so if something just will not come apart, look closely and see if it has reverse threads.

See **Tip 60**, bicycles

Grease here and back too

With electrical problems, you will find dirt, broken wires, or poor connections, 90% of the time. Look for the obvious. Check the breaker box in your house, and fuses in electric stoves. Check the wire right at the plug. They usually break there. Sometimes the insulation makes it look like it is not broken. Cut the plug off, and replace it. See: **Tip 76**, replacing a plug.

Rarely you will find carbon arcing. This is a line of carbon on an electrical part. Usually found on old appliances.

The line of carbon was not part of the appliance, but grew there over time. It conducts electricity from the proper terminal of the part, to ground, and causes a short. Scrape, or sand it off, and it will work fine.

Electric stove top elements will stop working when the plug in part, on the element, gets worn. Try twisting the end of the plug in part to get a tighter fit. If that fails, buy a new receptacle, and if necessary, a new element. See: **Tip 77**, appliance parts.

Gas stoves have electronic igniters. When they fail, use matches, or a hand held barbeque lighter. If you buy a new one, it will fail too.

Home appliances run on 110 volt, AC. This electricity WILL hurt, or kill you. Never work on a home appliance unless it is unplugged.

If you allow the "hot" black wire to touch the green "ground" wire, it should trip a circuit breaker at the breaker box.

If your body is not grounded, then touching the hot black wire will not hurt, or kill you. There is only one way to find out if you are grounded, don't do it.

TIP 071 ▸ GREASE YOUR APPLIANCES

When squeaks or slow running happen, apply grease. Use regular grease, or aerosol white grease for hard to reach places.

When you get a household appliance open, find where it was originally greased. Wipe off the old grease, and put more there. Put it where the squeak is.

Some appliances have rubber belts that need special grease.
See **Tip 77**, buying parts for appliances.

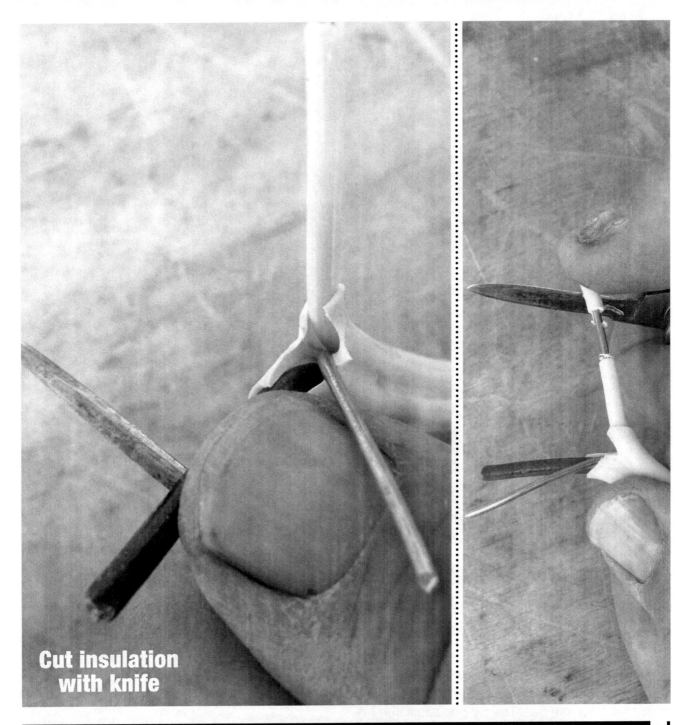

Cut insulation with knife

RE-NEW ELECTRICAL CONNECTIONS

072

TIP

Cut the wire. Strip the insulation. Leave just enough wire sticking out of the insulation to make the connection, or it might short out, make sparks, and send you to the electrical panel to re-set the breaker.

A blown circuit breaker is easily spotted. The little switch is in between "on" and "off."
Re-set it by turning it off, then on again.

073 ▷ BELT DRESSING AND BELT ADJUSTMENT

If your riding lawn mower, makes a squealing sound, when mowing, it is because a belt is loose. A belt adjustment may or may not be possible. Usually you have to replace the belt. The old one has a number on it, and the Owner's Manual will tell you the part number. Any good auto parts place can get a new one for you.

However, you can extend the life of that belt with belt dressing. Buy a can of Permatex belt dressing, and spray it on the moving belt. Watch those fingers! If the belt is new, and the mower old, you may have a bearing that is in need of grease. See: **Tips 12** *and* **125,** about bearings, and greasing them.

TILLER

AIR FILTER

START THAT LAWN MOWER OR TILLER FIRST PULL   ◄ 074 TIP

If it was running last time you used it in the fall, it will start, but might need some help first time in the spring.

Go buy some starter fluid. There are many brand names, but all contain ether. Squirt some on the air filter, and give a pull. Use more if it does not start the first or second pull.

To make sure your lawnmower or tiller is ready to start, in the spring, store it with the piston at the top of the cylinder. To find this spot, pull the rope slowly until you feel the resistance of the "compression" stroke.

By leaving the piston at the top, the valves will be closed, and the risk of one sticking open in the spring is eliminated. If you forget, and a valve does stick open, you will know it is stuck, because there is no "compression" stroke. Take out the spark plug, and push the stuck valve closed, with a screwdriver.

Pull the rope slowly a couple of times to rotate the engine, while pushing gently on the stuck valve.

Some small engines have an "easy pull" feature, which "relaxes" the compression stroke. However, it is still there.

See if you can get a mid 80's Maytag washer and dryer. Or other major appliances made in the mid 1980s. They last forever, with minor repairs.

Do not believe the crap about how the old ones are less "energy efficient" than new ones. With a new washer, there maybe some savings because of lower water use, but if the machine is junk in 5 years, there is no savings at all.

Go to second hand stores, garage sales, or Value Village, and buy appliances, like electric kettles, toasters, or mechanical things like clocks and timers, that were manufactured BEFORE 1985. Chances are, with a small repair, they will last way longer than the junk on the market today.

To give you an idea about the size of the problem, there were 673,000 searches on Google in July 2011 for: "appliance repair."

If you want new appliances, visit one of the websites devoted to reviews of new appliances, by people that own them, or look at Consumer Reports. This will help in the decision process. Paying $26 per year to Consumer Reports is a bargain compared to buying a poorly made major appliance that quits in 5 years, and cannot be fixed.

The "best appliance at the best price" does not mean the cheapest price. It means the price per year that it costs you. If the Federal Government really was on our side, they would require a sticker, with an estimated "Capital Cost per Year." This would be an estimate of how long the thing will work before it breaks down.

Same idea as the EnerGuide requirement in Canada, which requires a sticker that tells the consumer the estimated annual energy consumption of major appliances.

For example, suppose you were considering two equally good looking washing machines, one that cost $1,000, and the other $2,000. The "Capital Cost per Year" sticker says that the $1,000 washer would cost $300 per year, and the $2,000 washer would cost $100 per year, which would you buy? Which one would a bank finance on a five year term?

Call your Congressman or Member of Parliament today. I am sure they will get right on it!

Cut the old one off. Go buy a new one, with the same number of prongs, ie 2 or 3. Strip the insulation off of the wires, with an insulation stripper.

Use the leverage between your index finger, and the tool to get the insulation off, after you cut it with the tool.

Twist the copper strands of the wire together, so you can connect it to the new plug. Some new plugs have screw on connections. Make a small loop in the end of the wire, and attach it to the new plug with the screw.

Two things are important. First, cut the insulation back only as far as necessary to expose the wire to be attached to the screw. Second, put the loop on so that when the screw is tightened clockwise, the loop will tighten, not open.

There are only 3 wires possible on 110/120 volt appliances. Black, white, and green. The green is ground, it goes on the round plug prong. It doesn't really matter about the black and white. Either can go onto either plug prong, although on some plugs, one prong is fatter than another.

The green is supposed to attach to the metal frame of the appliance, if it has one, so that if there is an internal short, the electricity goes into the green wire, and to ground, and not into you. The green wire, if there is one, is connected to a round blade that goes into the wall.

If there is a bare wire, it too is a ground wire. If you are attaching something to household electrical, the bare wire in the wall connects to the green wire, or fitting on the thing you are installing.

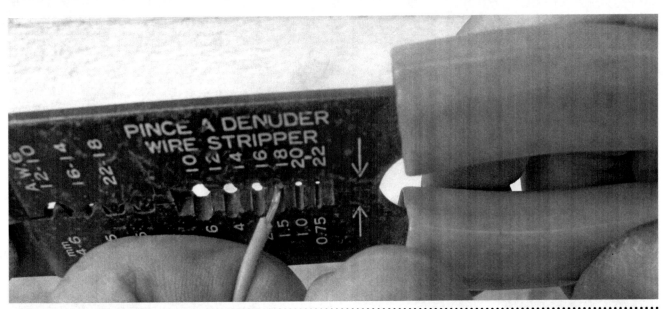

When the screw is tightened the loop of wire gets tighter

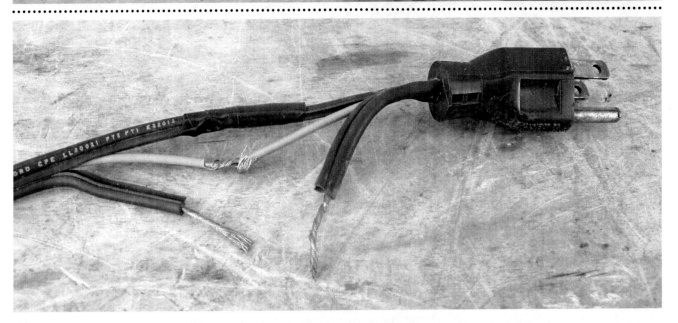

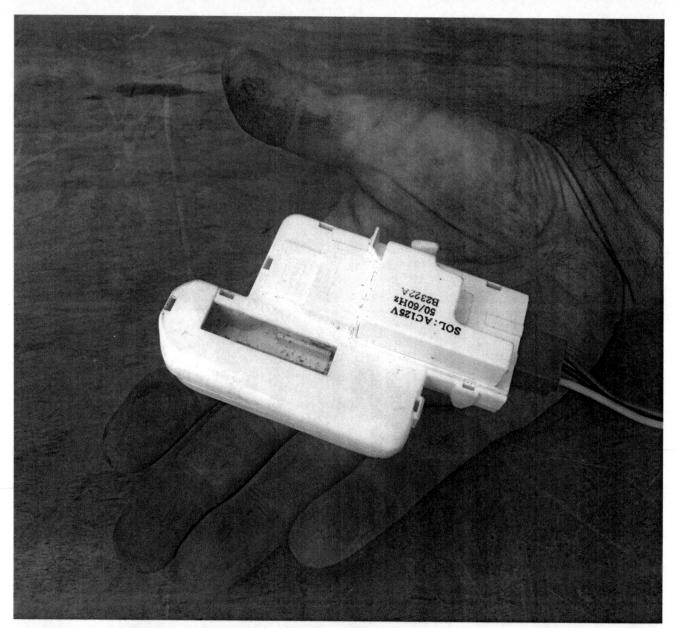

Parts from the manufacturer will be the most expensive. Try the "aftermarket" suppliers first. Look on the net, or in the Yellow Pages under "appliances."

In most cities there are companies that supply parts for almost every major appliance. If you need a timer for your dryer, or a belt for your dishwasher, they will have it, and at far less cost than the dealer.

You should find the model number, and serial number of the appliance, when calling around. On major appliances, the model number is on a little plate, or sticker somewhere. Other things will have the model number in the Owners Manual.

Always have the old part in your hand when you go for the new one.

GENERAL

On the night in 1865 when President Abraham Lincoln was assassinated at Ford's Theater he had a pair of glasses, among other things, in his pockets. The glasses were gold rimmed, and one of the bows, or arms was held on with a piece of string.

REMOVING SOMETHING THAT IS PRESSED ONTO A SHAFT

Use two screwdrivers, or anything else that can fit under the part to be removed. Apply pressure evenly on both sides, or it will not come straight off. A little oil, or WD 40 on the shaft helps. If you cannot get it started, tap lightly on the end of the shaft with a hammer. Three hands helps for this last step.

See **Tip 139**, removing things with a gear puller.

GASKET

PUNCH

2X4

079 ► MAKING A NEAT PUNCHED HOLE

Put a short piece of 2x4 on end to support hole punching.

A punch like this can be made from a piece of copper or steel tube. See: **Tip 113**, making tools.

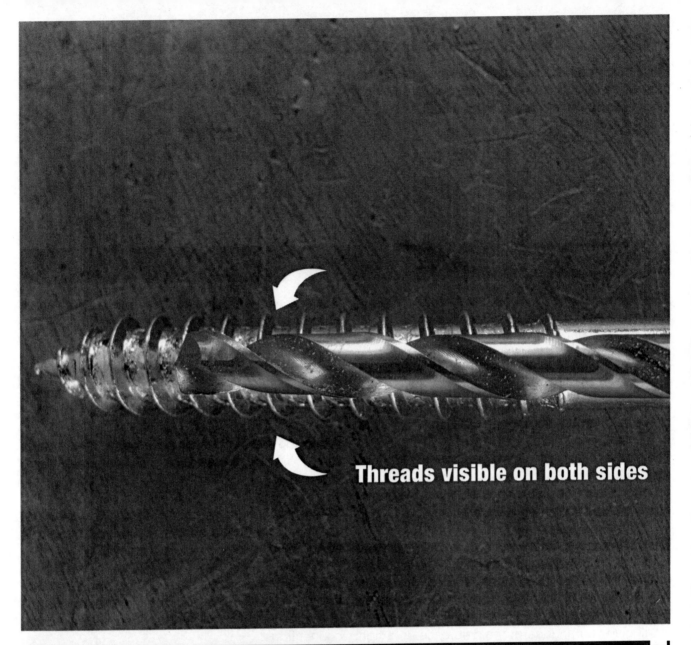

Threads visible on both sides

Hold the screw, or rivet, behind the bit. The bit should be larger than the diameter of the rivet, or the diameter of the screw, ignoring the threads on a screw.

This is an example of a wood screw, and drill bit.

Drill a test hole, and see if you have the right bit.

See: **Tip 109**, selecting drill bits for machine threads.

See **Tip 141**, drilling holes in metal.

Use a heavy hammer to absorb the blows of a lighter one, when driving nails in a flimsy board. Having a helping hand on this one is a good idea.

Your nose will help you figure out all sorts of things. Gasoline smells completely different from diesel fuel, or alcohol. Paint thinner and methyl hydrate have completely different smells. Burning brake pads, or clutch lining has a distinct smell. Brake fluid smells entirely different from power steering fluid. If you cannot figure out which reservoir on your car has brake fluid, go buy a can, and smell it.

The piston rings in an engine separate the lubricating oil in the crankcase from the burning fuel in the cylinder. When the piston rings are worn, the engine burns oil, and is nearing retirement age.

The smell and appearance of engine oil will tell you a lot about the condition of the piston rings inside the engine. If it is black, and smells burned, the engine is probably on its last legs. Smell the dipstick just after you change oil, and just before you change it. It will give you an idea of the difference. In a tight engine, there will not be much difference.

See: **Tip 26**, changing oil.

When shopping for a used car, a sniff of engine oil that has not been changed recently will tell you volumes about the condition of the engine. If it is not black, and does not smell burned, it has either been changed recently or it is a good engine.

Diesel engines almost always have black oil, and not much can be learned from it.

Power steering fluid is another one that will smell burned when it is overdue for a change.

See: **Tip 48**, replacing power steering fluid.

A container may have one label, and a different substance inside, but your nose knows.

When the rubber belt on your riding lawnmower slips too much, there will be a distinct smell: burning rubber.

When your car engine gets really hot, you will smell it. When that cheap shop vacuum you bought is about to self destruct, you will smell it.

Hot automotive grease has a distinct smell, as does the gas leaking out of your tank, or the acrid smell of the insulation burning off of your auto electrical connections.

Know what anti-freeze smells, and looks like, so when a puddle appears under your car, you can identify it. Go sniff and look under your radiator cap, when the engine is COLD.

You can tell cedar from Douglas fir, or pine, just by smelling it. If an engine is made of cedar, do not buy the car.

Do not spend much time sniffing gasoline or solvents, or you will go crazy. Do not stick your nose right into the container. Use your hand to "wave" the fumes towards your nose.

This hammer absorbs the impact

TIP 083 ▷ READ THE MANUAL

I said this in **Tip 39**. This is really important.

The manufacturer will give you important information about your machine. How it goes together, and comes apart, but most importantly, how to care for it. Some manuals are better than others, but just about everything you buy will have some sort of manual.

TIP 084 ▷ KNOW WHEN YOU ARE IN OVER YOUR HEAD

This one is tough. As a Terminal Optimist, I never quit. However, when the next step you take may endanger the existence of the machine, you may wish to re-consider, and call for help.

See: **Tip 97**. Go for lunch, and think about the problem.

Cut the stuck hose

Cut off the stuck part

EASY REMOVAL OF STUCK RUBBER HOSES

085 TIP

Usually there is enough extra to stretch the 1/2 to 3/4 inch or so, length of the fitting. Eyeball it, then cut the hose off with side cutters. Use a razor blade knife to split the stuck piece so you can remove it.

Re-install with spit.

See **Tip 136**, Spit and Bailing wire.

Shoot grease at joint

086 ▶ GREASE EVERYTHING

Grease is the cure all for a vast number of problems.
2 cents worth of grease can save hundreds of dollars to replace burned out parts. When something is
squeaking or running slow, take it apart and grease it.

If you delay, better put in for overtime. One sunroof,
or window motor on a modern car can cost $500.

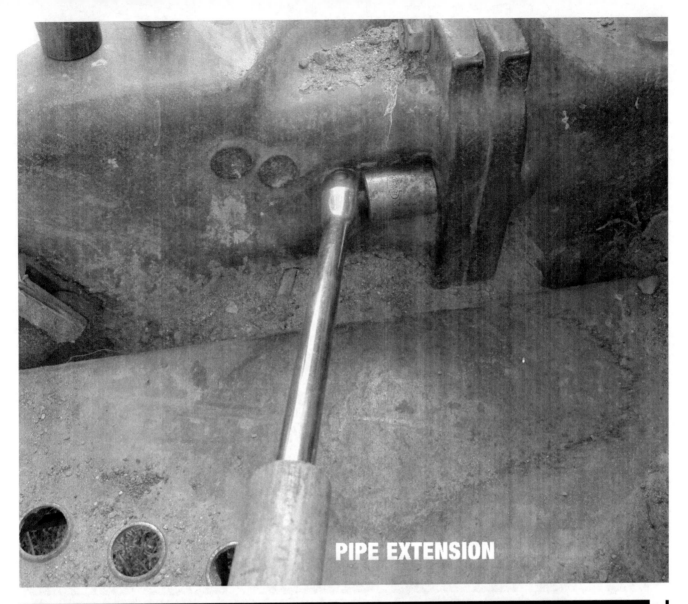

PIPE EXTENSION

INCREASE THE POWER OF YOUR HAND TOOLS

Make a "helper handle" to increase the leverage of a tool.

Put a pipe over the end of a good quality breaker bar to increase torque. Apply pressure slowly. Do not jerk it. Pound the head of the bolt, or the nut to jar the threads before trying to break it loose with the breaker bar. Apply penetrating oil.

Never put anything together this way, unless you are really familiar with the amount of torque you are applying. See: **Tip 114**, tightening things.

See: **Tip 119**, buying tools.

Rent a torque wrench for the day to find out about torque. See **Tip 42**, about torque wrenches.

PLUMBER'S TORCH

Stuck nut

088 ▷ HOW TO USE HEAT TO HELP TAKE THINGS APART

Getting two parts to separate is easier if one part expands slightly. Heat the "outside" part, usually the nut, to expand it. Apply WD 40 or some other penetrating oil. Twist it before the "inside part", usually the bolt, gets hot, or the advantage is lost.

Use a plumber's propane torch. The hottest part of the flame is at the tip.

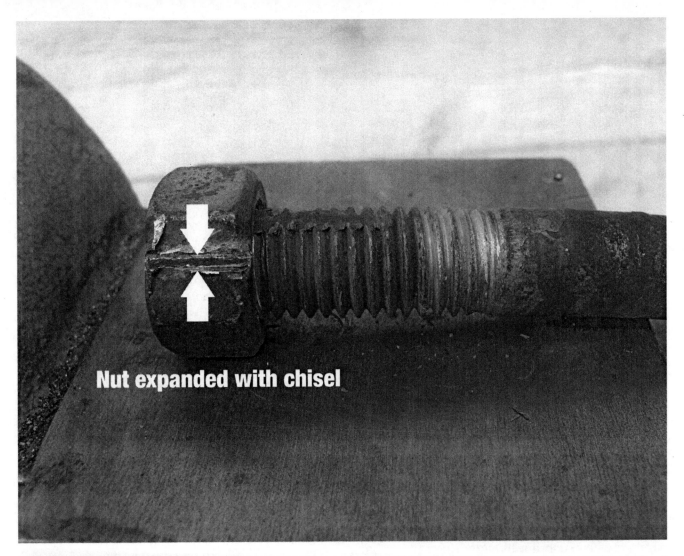

Nut expanded with chisel

The objective is to "enlarge" the nut, by stretching it. It needs to be replaced after this treatment.

Nut takes the force of hammer

NEW WASHER

TIP 090 ▶ UNSCREWING SOMETHING IS NOT A ONE WAY STREET

After heating a nut, slowly un-screw it by going ½ turn off, and then back on again. Apply penetrating oil, then wire brush the threads. Keep going back and forth until it is free. If you do not, sometimes the friction will build up, and something may break.

TIP 091 ▶ USING A NUT TO TAKE HAMMER BLOWS ON END OF SHAFT/BOLT

Sometimes a bolt or shaft will not come free after removal of the nut. To get it free, put the nut back on, leaving a 1/8 inch gap, and hit it with a hammer.

As the bolt moves out, unscrew the nut a bit, and continue to hit it as necessary. The force of the hammer blows on the nut will keep the end of the bolt or shaft from "mushrooming." The shaft or bolt may be impossible to remove, if the end has mushroomed, but it is a certainty that it will be impossible to put the nut back on.

Usually you will need a new nut.

If the nut is damaged, it will not go onto the shaft all the way, and there may be a gap. Fill it with a washer.

See: **Tips 92** and **93**, for ways to clean up the threads, if you live in the country, and cannot get a new nut right away.

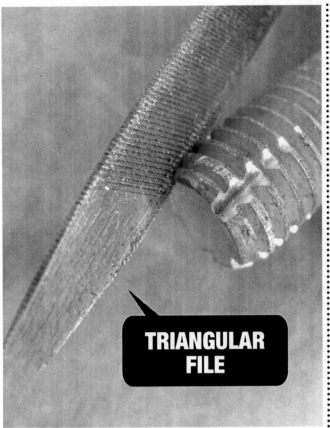

TRIANGULAR FILE

NUT

MAKE A TOOL TO REPAIR DAMAGED THREADS

092 TIP

Cleaning up threads with a home made tap and die set is easy. A tap cuts threads in a hole, and a die cuts threads on a rod.

Cut grooves into the end of the bolt, or inside of the nut, with a triangular file. Twist the nut or bolt back and forth, over the damaged threads, applying light oil, or cutting oil. Remove the metal shavings.

If you wear one of these home made tools out, make a new one. If the nut or bolt you use to make a tap or die is needed to reassemble the machine, use it.

093   ANOTHER WAY TO REPAIR DAMAGED THREADS

Sometimes a fitting, or other part is in a tight place. Or, the fitting does not take a nut. Like hydraulic fittings. Use a triangular file to restore threads. The very first thread is most important, because it leads all the rest.

See: **Tip 92**, making a tool to repair damaged theads.

Use a socket to install bushing

Use a socket to install seal

USE A SOCKET TO INSTALL A SEAL

Drive the seal back in with a socket and hammer, or
press with a vise, or both.

Lube rear bushing on electric motor

Seal with Dum Dum

095 ▷ MAGIC LIQUID THAT MAKES EVERYTHING WORK BETTER

WD 40 will fix, or extend the life of almost anything. My 86 Volvo, with 450,000 km. (270,000 miles), had both its clock and heater motor "rejuvenated" with this stuff. Both lasted until the car quit at 550,000 km.

Drill a small hole into the unit that is not working. Stick the little plastic pipe in, and give it a squirt. There is no risk, because it was not working, or working badly, anyway.

Afterwards, plug the hole with Dum Dum putty. It is called that because you are smart smart to ask for it at the auto parts place.

With electric motors, put the hole just beside the rear bushing. That is the one that squeaks. See: **Tip 12**, bearings and bushings.

When taking threaded things apart, start with a squirt, it makes everything go easier.

For really rusty or stuck parts, put some on, and let it soak overnight. You can also heat the part, with a plumber's torch, before or after applying WD40. The WD40 might catch fire. Not a big fire, just a little one.

SAVE YOUR KNUCKLES

TIP 096

Think about where your knuckles will end up if something you are pushing on slips. If you do not think about it, you may get a rude wake up call. Keep some Band Aids around.

THE PROBLEM YOU CANNOT SOLVE

TIP 097

Go have lunch and think about it.

Often the answer is right there, but because of fatigue, frustration or ego you cannot see it. Take a time out to meditate on the problem over lunch. The answer will appear.

WIRE BRUSH THREADS

TIP 098

Clean threads go together better. Give a rusty or dirty bolt a few strokes with the wire brush, and apply a bit of oil. It will go back together like new.

THE PART THAT WILL GO ON TWO DIFFERENT WAYS

TIP 099

A very rare problem, but it does come up. It came up for me with my lawn tractor. The main drive belt for the mower blades, will go on two different ways. The wrong way allows it to slip, and no amount of belt dressing will make it quiet.

If I had paid attention to how it came off, and/or read the manual, I would not have had the problem. I finally did read the manual, and the diagram of how the belt goes on, had lunch, and figured it out.

LOCKING THREADED THINGS

TIP 100

Use Loctite, or another similar thread locking product, if a lock washer is impractical, or, if you have a lock washer, and you are really anal, and want to make FOR SURE, FOR SURE, it does not come loose.

See: **Tip 107**, washer pile ups.

Tapered pipe thread

101 ▷ UNDERSTANDING THREADS

There are: pipe, fine, coarse, and metric threads. There are also wood screws.

Wood screws can be used for sheet metal. **Tip 80** shows a wood screw.

Pipe threads are tapered, so that the fitting automatically tightens up. Not found on cars.

Machine threads come in coarse and fine.

Metric threads are different than standard threads.

Machines have both metric and standard threads these days. Even machines built in North America may have metric nuts bolts, and threads.

If a bolt and nut will not go together, past the first two or three threads, you may have a mismatch of metric and standard.

GRADE 5

GRADE 2

Not all hardware is created equal. There are soft "stove" bolts, and super hard, heavy duty equipment bolts. Most automotive bolts are grade 2 or 5. Inside an engine, or differential, harder, grade 7 or higher bolts may be found.

The difference is written on the head of the bolt.

Metric bolts have numbers rather than marks. The higher the number, the harder it is.

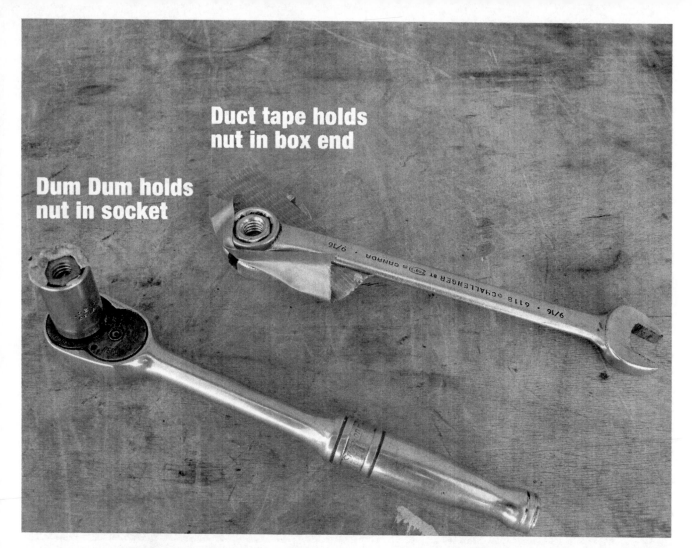

**Duct tape holds
nut in box end**

**Dum Dum holds
nut in socket**

TIP 103 ▷ GETTING A NUT INTO AN IMPOSSIBLE SPOT

Use Dum Dum putty (get it at an auto parts store)
to hold a nut in socket. Yes, that is what it is called.
Your auto parts guys will know what you want.

Use duct tape to hold a nut in box end wrench.

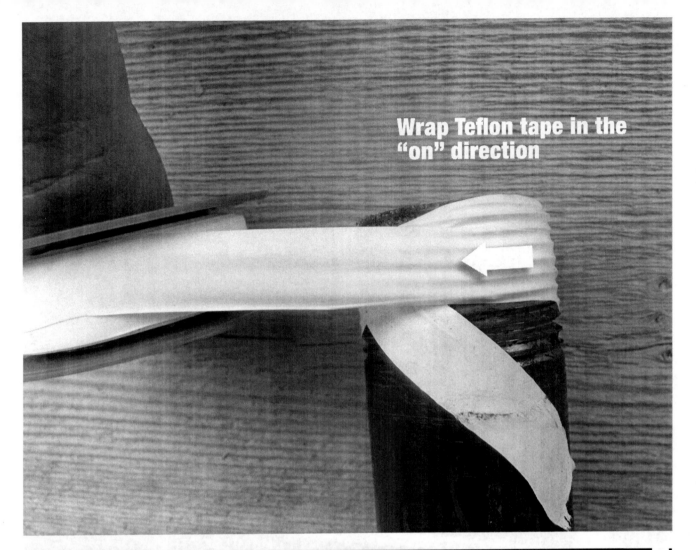

Wrap Teflon tape in the "on" direction

MAKING FITTINGS LEAK PROOF

Make sure threads on water, oil or gas connections do not leak.

Wrap the threads with Teflon tape. Wind it onto the threads, with the "on" direction of the threads, so it does not unwind when you screw it into the other part.

Punch aligns parts

SPEED NUT

105 — ALIGNING PARTS SO YOU CAN BOLT THEM TOGETHER

When trying to connect two pieces with a bolt, the two pieces can be aligned with a drift punch. Also works to align a speed nut so you can put the screw into it.

Use a drift punch, with a straight shaft, of the proper diameter, to align the holes. Or for a speed nut, a center punch will work better. See: **Tip 9** photo.

If there are several bolts that have to be put in, you can also do a "preliminary assembly" with only the bolt and nut. Now you can draw the two parts together, put in more bolts, with proper washer pile ups, and a nut, then go back and add the washers to the first one.

See: **Tip 107**, washer pile ups.

SELF LOCKING NUT

Machine is here

FLAT WASHER

LOCK WASHER

WIGGLE IT 106

Threads need a bit of wiggling sometimes to come loose, or go together. A bit of oil helps too.

PROPER WASHER PILE UPS 107

Use a flat washer between the bolt head and machine. On the other side of the machine, flat washer, lock washer, nut.

You can leave out the lock washer if a self locking nut is used. These nuts have a nylon insert that grips the threads of the bolt so it does not unscrew.

Punch bushing out from other side

108 ▷ USE A PUNCH TO DRIVE THINGS OUT

Bearings, bushings, and seals inside a machine are easily removed with a drift punch. Tap around the edge, in a circular pattern, to keep the part moving straight.

There may be a "lip" on the inside, that the bearing or seal sits on. Do not try to drive that out.

See: **Tip 9**, using a punch or chisel.

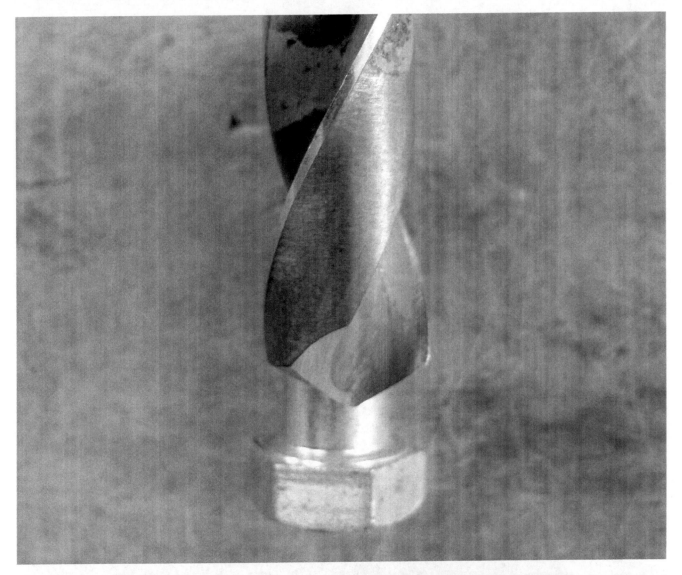

SELECTING THE RIGHT SIZE DRILL BIT FOR A MACHINE BOLT

Hold the drill bit in front of the bolt. The drill should completely cover the bolt, at the shoulder, which is the widest part. Drill a test hole.

This is different from the procedure in **Tip 80**. With machine bolts, the threads, and shoulder, must pass through the hole, not bite into it.

Practice engine

110 ▷ TAKE IT APART SO YOU CAN PUT IT BACK TOGETHER AGAIN

Mark things as they come apart. Use a triangular file, punch, or paint stick. Or pile up parts in the order they came off.

It is also helpful, with a really complicated thing, to partly disassemble, then re-assemble it, loosely, then take it apart again. Train your brain.

You are also free to take notes about how it came apart. There will be a test!

First layer is the sheet metal or outer body of the machine. Next are the individual components, such as the fuel pump, the starter, the manifold. Label the containers if necessary, because at the end, those fuel pump bolts may look just like the manifold bolts, but are 1/8 inch too short.

First layer comes off

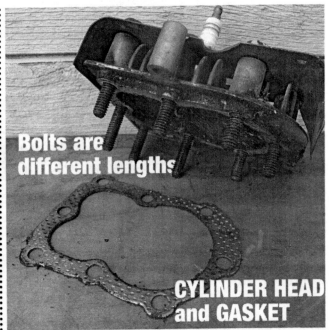

Bolts are different lengths

CYLINDER HEAD and GASKET

Tap the housing gently

111 ▷ ALWAYS PUT HARDWARE IN CONTAINERS

Much time is wasted looking for a nut on the ground. Hubcaps, when cars still had them, were great for lug nuts. Keep a few yogurt containers, old baking pans, milk carton bottoms or tin cans around to use.

112 ▷ LOOSENING THREADS

Tap things to loosen threads. Soak with penetrating oil.

Use a hammer to whack the head of a bolt. It will jar the threads. Use penetrating oil. Leave over night if really old and rusty. If really really rusty, see **Tip 88**, heating things.

113 ▷ MAKING TOOLS

There are lots of tools you can make out of wire, aluminum, copper pipe, and other things.

Make a jumper wire out of two alligator clips and a piece of wire. Use it to bypass electrical things you think are faulty.

For example, if you think the safety switch on the lawn mower seat is broken, bypass it, with the jumper wire. See if the mower will work. Then you know what to fix.

Make a pilot shaft, or short wrenches by cutting with grinder.

This is a tip for the more experienced mechanic. Clutch pressure plates must be aligned with the bearing in the flywheel or mating the engine to the manual transmission will be impossible. Use a cut off transmission shaft as a tool to align these things.

Make new tools out of old ones.

Make a punch out of tubing, by filing the end. Cut a short piece of copper or steel tube, and file an edge on one end. You can now use it to cut holes. Place the material to be punched onto a piece of wood, end grain up.

Shaft cut to fit 3/4 inch drill

SIX POINT SOCKET

15/16 GRAY CANADA

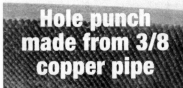

Hole punch made from 3/8 copper pipe

Cut the edge with an axe file

Use chainsaw file to file the burr off the inside

JUMPER WIRE

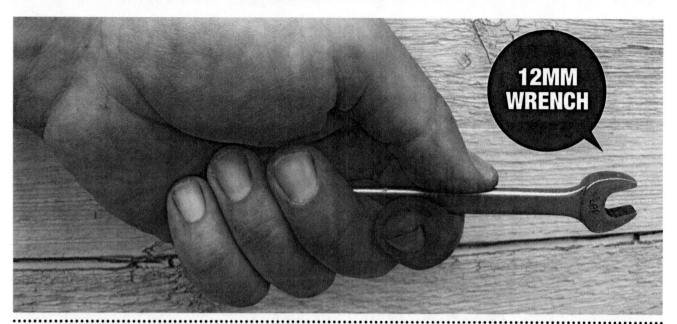

12MM WRENCH

22MM WRENCH

TIP **114** HOW TO TORQUE (OR TIGHTEN) THINGS

Use the length of the wrench as a guide. First timers usually over tighten.

Every wrench gets longer as the size gets bigger. The amount of torque needed to keep a nut or bolt tight usually increases with the diameter of the nut or bolt.

So, if you apply about the same pressure to a wrench for a 12mm bolt, as you do for a 22mm bolt, you will be about right, assuming you do not strip the smallest one.

See **Tip 137**, practice breaking things.

See **Tip 42**, rent a torque wrench for a day.

Round jaws

Flat jaws

Vice Grips. Use them to hold things, bring two parts together, grip things.

When trying to assemble something, especially in tight quarters, holding the parts together with vice grips makes it easier to insert the bolt, and proper washer pile up before putting on the nut.

They are most useful when there is nothing left of the slot in a screw, or the flat surfaces on a nut or bolt. The locking mechanism in the handle grabs the part far tighter than you could squeeze.

Welding would be impossible without them. The pieces of metal you want to weld together can be held with Vice Grips until that first bead is on.

See: **Tip 118**, cheap tools.

See **Tip 132**.

Grind new flats on bolt head

| 116 | THE BOLT HEAD THAT IS ROUNDED |

Make new flats on the bolt head

Use an axe file, grinder, or other metal file to make new flat surfaces for your wrench.

It will be almost impossible to file the bolt or nut to an exact size, so a 1/2 inch, or 13mm socket will fit. Just get two opposing flats, flat, and use an end wrench, or crescent wrench.

If this fails, use the hammer and chisel approach, see: **Tip 127**.

If the hammer and chisel approach fails, see: **Tip133**.

THE INDENTED PLUG OR SCREW THAT IS STRIPPED

Use a punch to turn a plug or screw that is set flush
(level) with the part it holds, or where the flats have
become impossible to put a wrench on. Use the
punch instead of a chisel, for example, where the
part you want to turn is soft, like brass.

Torque, or tighten the part evenly. Where there are more than 3 bolts or nuts holding two things together, you must tighten it evenly. Although it is made of metal, it does warp when tightened down.

No matter how simple the machine, when you put it back together, adopt a crisscross, or circular pattern of tightening.

For a long thing like a cylinder head, start in the middle, and tighten in a circular pattern, outwards.

For the lug nuts on your car's wheels, tighten the first one, then the opposite one, then the next opposite one, etc.

Tighten a bit first time around, then tighten for keeps the second time around.

NEVER buy cheap tools. They will always break just when you need them the most, or they simply will not work properly. Most auto parts places carry cheap and good tools. 40 wrenches for $9.95 is a disaster waiting to happen.

The hammer pictured in **Tip 14**, is marked "Shopro Professional", and has an indication that the name is a Registered Trademark. It is unknown at the US or Canadian Trademark offices, and Google has no results for the name. There are no markings saying where it was made. It is a piece of junk. The rounded face guarantees it will not drive nails properly. It was cheap, but it has a nice shiny finish, and looks good.

NEVER buy tools made in China, even with a warranty. They are not as good as tools made in North America, Germany or Sweden. If a tool does not say where it was made, you can assume some back alley shop in Guangdong, made it.

Check out pawn shops, and flea markets. That is where all the stolen tools go. Buy brand names. Get them way cheaper second hand. I still have tools I bought 29 years ago. The ones I had 30 years ago got stolen.

See **Tip151**, marking your tools.

Snap-on, are probably the best. Proto Industrial, and Gray are excellent, and Sears Craftsman not bad. I say "not bad", because they are just a bit clunkier than the others, but are guaranteed for life, and work well. Plus, there are lots of stores to return them to, if they break.

If you cannot get a "lifetime replacement" guarantee, on a tool, it means the company that made the tool has little confidence in it, so why should you?

There is one exception on the Chinese tool rule. Some items have to meet North American safety standards. Also, heavy industrial items, like bench vises can be OK.

"Consumer grade" Chinese tools are the ones to avoid. Even if they have a recognized brand name, they are to be avoided.

Using cheap Chinese tools to fix a broken Chinese made product is a sure path to insanity.

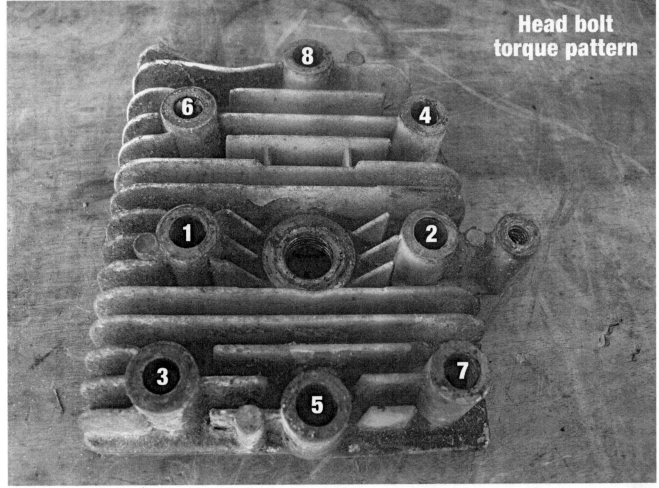

Head bolt torque pattern

120 ▶ **CREATING FIXES OUT OF RANDOM PARTS**

Keep lots of spare nuts, bolts and washers around.

Also pieces of pipe, tubing, metal of all descriptions, may all come in handy. The best home mechanics, and do-it-yourselfers, have a great junk collection. Learn what is metric, what is standard. All Asian and European machines are metric. Most US and Canadian are standard. But there are exceptions in the US and Canada.

Because of global trade, you might find that the starter or alternator on your tractor is Japanese, miscellaneous items are made in Spain, while the basic unit is made in the US, with standard threads.

Make collections of nuts and bolts, washers, pins, odds and ends. And anything with a thread should be labeled, "Metric" or "Standard."

Keep your parts where you can find them. I use lots of different containers, including an old snail mail box. Your spouse may think it is messy to have all this junk around, but will be happy when you fix something with it. I once got a huge collection of random parts, complete with cans, at an estate sale. The guy had died, and his junk went cheap. Most of the cans were tobacco cans. Guess what he died of.

The thermostat housing on my 95 Volvo is presently held on with a 10mm nut from a junk bicycle, made in Japan. That nut made the car drivable, after I wrecked the original nut while replacing the thermostat. Since I live in the country, and have only one car, that one nut saved me a lot of trouble.

When something is ready for the trash, take off any nuts, bolts, fasteners that you can, and put them in labeled containers, i.e. "metric" or "standard."

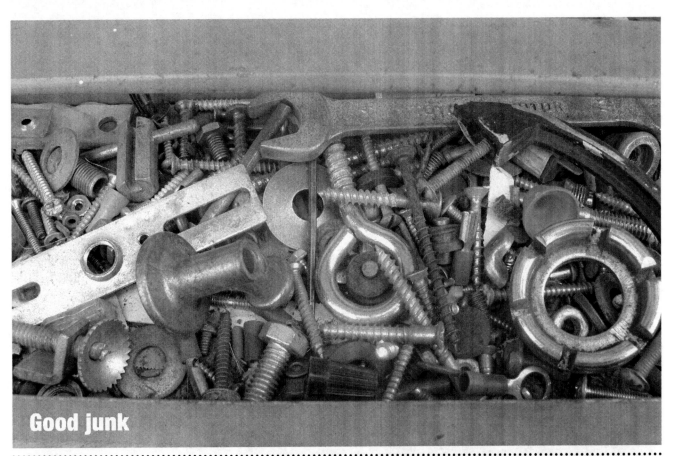

Good junk

T. Ross J. Stevenson M. Williams

R. Roy T. Tagami K. Weremchuk

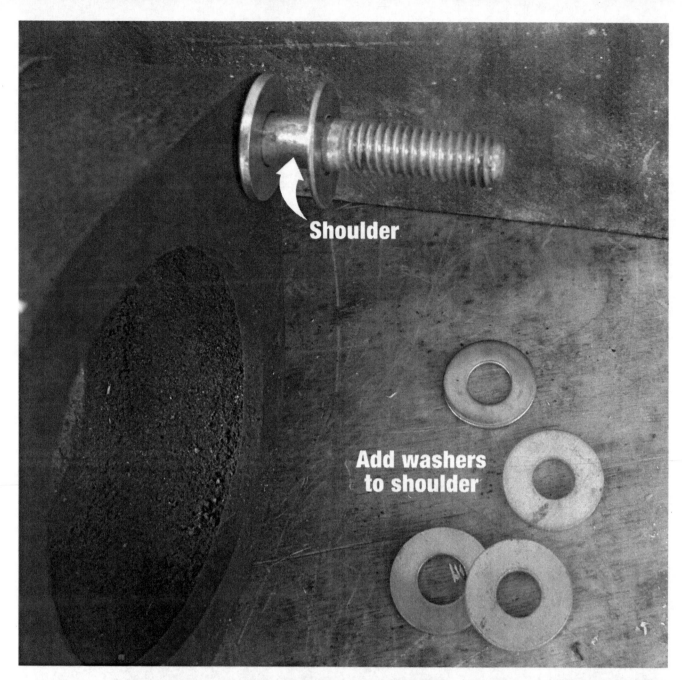

Shoulder

Add washers to shoulder

121 USING WASHERS TO TAKE UP SLACK

Excess space on a shaft? Use a washer, or two.
Keep a bunch in the shop for these emergencies.

HACKSAW

THE BOLT THAT IS TOO LONG

The replacement bolt from your hardware collection, or the hardware store, may be to long. Cut it shorter with a hacksaw, but before you do, put a nut on it. Then after the cut, take the nut off. It will clean up the threads.

If you forget to put the nut on, see **Tips 92** and **93**, cleaning up threads.

Tighten the nuts together

123   USE TWO NUTS LOCKED TOGETHER TO TURN SHAFT

Put the first nut on the shaft, and leave room for the second. Then put the second nut on, and twist them together. This makes a strong point for twisting the shaft.

It can also be used for locking a bolt or shaft in place, so it will not come loose.

Bungee cord replaces spring on lawn mower

BUNGEE CORDS AND DUCT TAPE

Bungee cords can replace springs in all sorts of things. They can also hold things down, or hold things together. They are a bit like bailing wire. Buy a selection, and keep them in your shop.

Duct tape will patch up holes in the plastic cases of the appliances you dissemble, and will hold all sorts of things together.

I once saw a young woman, in the parking lot of a hardware store, kid in the car seat, duct taping her Dodge Colt back together. Dash board, seats, and even the bumper cover. I really admired her spunk.

Also, see **Tip 136**, spit and bailing wire

BALL BEARING

Press grease from below

Packed ball bearing full of grease

Any ball bearing or roller bearing can be cleaned and re-packed with grease.

See **Tip 12**, ball and roller bearings.

Anything you buy that is made in China, and has bearings, needs to be greased, as soon as it comes out of the box.

I recently saw a nearly new Chinese made washing machine with a burned out ball bearing. The whole unit was junked. The managers who tell the workers at the People's Factories to skimp on the grease are committing a true economic crime, a crime against us.

First, remove the bearing. Clean with solvent. Get a glob of grease in your hand. Force the grease through the bearing, from the bottom. Spin it now and then to work it in.

When finished, the whole bearing should be full of grease

You do not need any special grease. Just ordinary "grease gun" grease will do.

Many ball bearings are "sealed". But these seals can be pried out with a small screwdriver, or knife,

so you can repack it with grease. Spray carburetor cleaner can be used to clean it. Press the grease through from the front. You cannot buy a new seal, so take it apart carefully. If you ruin the seal, make a new one of stiff paper, or flat plastic, like the kind a plastic milk jug is made of.

Roller bearings are found in places where there is maximum weight or heat, such as the wheel bearings on your car. The seals can be pried out, and re-used if you are careful. Re-pack the bearing the same way. Press the grease through from the bottom with your hand.

See: **Tip 18**, removing a wheel bearing seal

See **Tip 94**, using a socket to drive things in.

Seal removal

Seal removed

Use the chisel
to drive the head
counter clockwise

126 ▶ **REMOVING THE WORST NUTS AND BOLTS**

Use a grinder with a cutting wheel, or Dremel tool,
(for really tiny hardware) to take off the worst nuts.
As the Red Queen said: "Off with their heads".

See: **Tip 3**, the grinder.

127 ▶ **REMOVING PARTS WITH A CHISEL**

"Cold chisels" come in various sizes. They are used
on metal parts, especially thin parts, like exhaust
systems, and oil filters.

They are also used to crack nuts, and remove bolts
that have no flats left.

Part needing gasket

GASKET PAPER

MAKING GASKETS

128

TIP

It is unusual these days to need to make a gasket, however, here is how you do it. Get some sheet gasket material at your local auto part store. Tell them what sort of gasket you need to make.

Lightly oil the surface of the part. Press it onto the gasket material to make a pattern. Mark around the outside of the part. Cut out the large spaces, with scissors, and punch out the bolt holes.

See: **Tip 113**, making punches.

Grease

129 ▷ **RE-ASSEMBLING THINGS**

If it needs lubrication, re-assemble with a bit of grease.

Any grease will do, even Vaseline, or olive oil. Obviously, if it is a high friction, high temperature item, get good quality automotive grease.

BUT if the part is meant to be dry, do not grease it. Like the disc brakes in your car.

Use your head on this one.

See **Tip 110**, taking it apart, so you can put it back together again

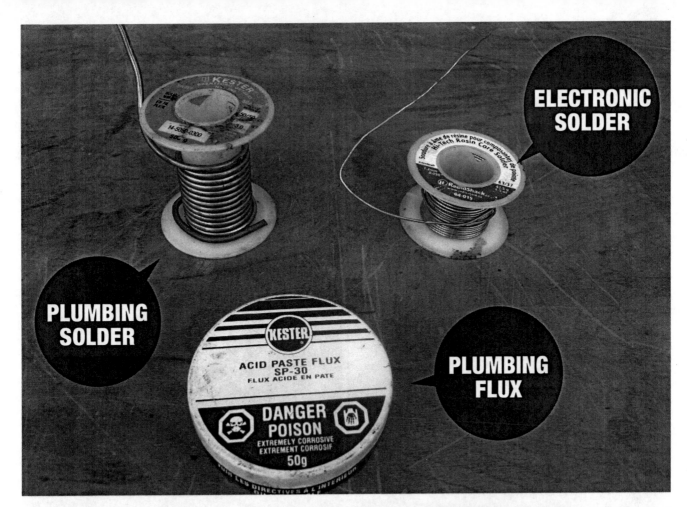

ELECTRONIC SOLDER

PLUMBING SOLDER

PLUMBING FLUX

KESTER
ACID PASTE FLUX
SP-30
FLUX ACIDE EN PATE

DANGER
POISON
EXTREMELY CORROSIVE
EXTREMENT CORROSIF
50g

(Pronounced: sod-er) So you won't sound dum dum when you go to the auto parts, or hardware store.

Solder is a lead, zinc product that comes in rolls that looks like wire. It is used to connect electrical wires, and for household copper plumbing. An electric soldering gun is used for wires, and a plumber's torch is used for copper plumbing.

There are two kinds of solder, and flux. Flux cleans the metal, and helps the solder stick.

Electronic solder has rosin flux. It is embedded in the solder. Smells like pine trees when melting. Use it for all electrical/electronic/automotive fixes. Rosin will not harm metal.

The other one is acid flux. Smells like poison. Comes in a small round can, and is used for plumbing. BE CAREFUL with this stuff. When soldering copper pipes, if you put more on than will burn off during soldering, it will sit there, and, over a few years, eat your plumbing, until you have an involuntary sprinkler system.

Wipe the pipes with a rag soaked in hot water after soldering.

Do not inhale the fumes.

When doing a repair on a household copper water pipe system, make sure all the water is out of the pipe, or you will never get it hot enough, with a plumber's torch, to melt the solder.

131 ▷ TIGHTENING AND LOOSENING THINGS

Unscrew counter clockwise, and tighten clockwise. Give it some thought when on your back looking up at something. See: **Tip 15,** clock photo.

The only exception to this is that rare machine, such as my Stihl weed whacker, and some cars made up to about 1970. Reverse threads were found on the right side of the wheels on the car. The weed whacker head on the Stihl has reverse threads.

Bike pedals, marked "L" for left hand threads.

Things with reverse threads will usually be marked, or it will be mentioned in the manual. If something just will not come apart, look closely and see if it has reverse threads.

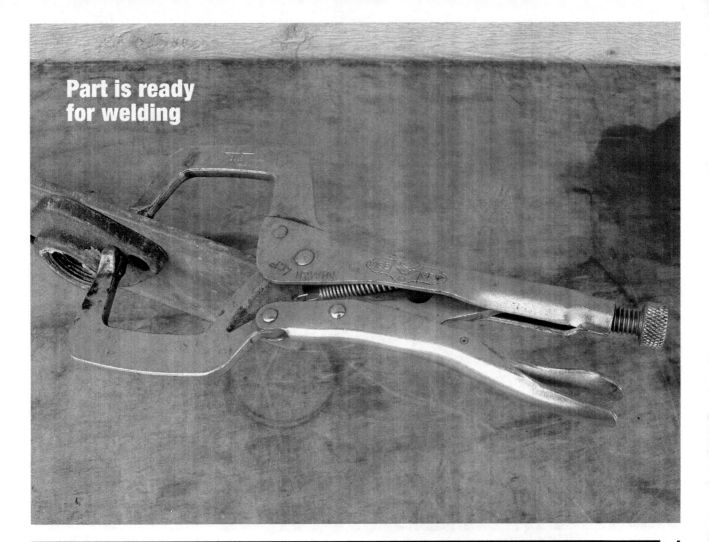

Part is ready for welding

GET SEVERAL SIZES OF VICE GRIPS

Some hardware is pathetic. Almost every screw I ever got with a Chinese product was crap. You need lots of vice grips to take them out, because the hex or slot will have disintegrated.

Buying good quality North American made replacement hardware is the next step. Or, look in your random parts collection. **Tip 120**.

See: **Tip 115**, the "must have" tool.

See: **Tip 133**, the stripped screw.

**Cut off ruined head
Remove with Vicegrips**

"EASY OUTS"

133 A STRIPPED SCREW YOU CANNOT GET OUT

Use your grinder to grind off the head. Then remove the part the screw was holding. Now you have a short stub of the screw to get a hold of. If you eventually destroy this without getting the screw out, you may have to drill a new hole, and add a new bolt and washer, if possible.

You can drill right through the old screw, or drill in a new spot, where the new bolt will fit.

Here is another idea. Drill right through the center of the cut off screw. Use an "easy out" to unscrew the remains of the screw.

The "easy out" usually has the drill size stamped on it.

They have sharp sides that cut into the remains of the cut off screw or bolt, when you twist them counter clockwise.

However you do it, do these things first: hit the head of the screw, or bolt with a hammer to jolt the threads. Second: apply penetrating oil, before and after hitting it. Let it sit over night.

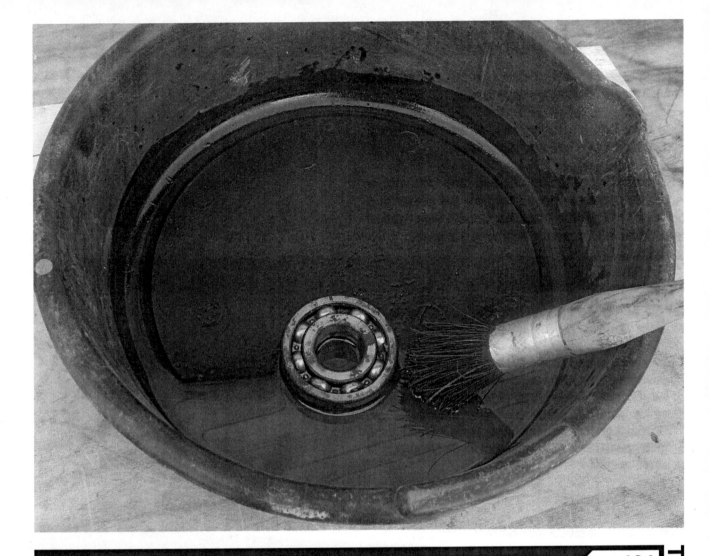

Use a parts brush either with solvent, or dry, to clean parts.

Dirt is the worst enemy of a machine. Even worse than bad mechanics, because it works slowly, and invisibly, until something breaks, and it is your fault.

Change oil and filters according to schedule. See: **Tips 39** and **83**, read the manual. When dismantling something, clean the parts with solvent or gasoline or paint thinner, or alcohol, (or whatever the manual says) depending on the machine.

Make sure you scrape every last bit of old gasket off, or the new one will leak. A putty knife is good for scraping gaskets.

Before you take a machine apart, brush off the dirt with the parts brush, preferably soaked in solvent, then blow with compressed air.

When a machine is apart, wrap things in rags to minimize dirt contact, and plug hose ends and open fittings with rags.

Change the oil right after any engine has been opened. Dirt always gets in.

Candle wax is both a bit sticky, and a bit slippery. It makes all sorts of things work better.

Use it for printers, or copiers, or wooden drawer slides. See if you can find other uses.

My printer/fax machine has two little soft rubber rollers that are supposed to grab the paper and shove it through the machine. Candle wax rubbed into those rollers greatly improves the grab.

An old expression, which has new relevance in our modern world of throw-away products.

Hay bailers, at one time used wire, instead of plastic twine. Farmers used the left over wire to make all sorts of things: replacement cotter pins, hangers for things, like a loose muffler, braces for broken wooden things. Wire is still good for many uses. Have several sizes around your house. Many different kinds are available at most hardware stores.

See: **Tip 124**, bungee cords and duct tape.

Spit is more useful than you may think. Sure it is necessary for chewing food, and fun pastimes between consenting adults, but if you want to slip a dry rubber hose over a steel tube, or nipple, or squeeze tight plastic parts together, spit is the best, and most convenient lubricant available.

Spit is also convenient for the end of "bright" (non-galvanized) nails to get them going in a piece of old, dry lumber. Do not put galvanized nails in your mouth.

Before you take apart a leaking tire, re-inflate it, and put a wad of spit on the end of the valve stem. You will see bubbles if it leaks. Tighten or replace it.

Here is my kettle, a really good one, except for one small rivet. When the rivet fell out, the kettle was unusable. Wire fixed it.

The little screws that hold the arms of your glasses on, fall out often. Wire will not fall out.

Rub candle wax
on two rollers

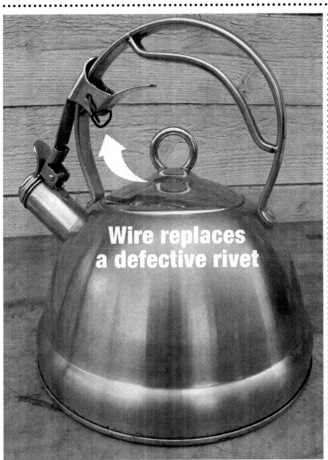
Wire replaces
a defective rivet

Wire holds
on arm

The only way you will get to know how much force to apply when turning or hitting things, is to practice, by apply too much force. Among the most common failures at fixing things is using to much force when re-assembling.

So, get a 3/8 bolt, for starters, and put a nut on it. Put it in a vise, and twist until it strips.

Whack a grade 2 bolt, then a grade 5 bolt with a ball peen hammer to see the damage.

See: **Tip 102**, about hardware grades.

When a difficult problem arises, set up a test on a similar part.

Let your destructive instincts run wild with spare parts. Then you will know how far you can go.

Pick up a dead lawn mower. Practice stripping threads, bashing aluminum casings, twisting the blade shaft, filing new flats on the bolts heads you rounded.

See: **Tip 116**, rounded bolt heads.

Be cautious and observe during disassembly. Look for punch marks, wear marks, paint remnants, or other clues about assembly. When you do that rubber timing belt on your car, you must line up the cam shaft with the crankshaft. There are marks for this purpose.

There are always clues. Best if you just pile up the parts as they come off. Leave these esoteric paint and wear marks for when you are desperate.

See: **Tip 110**, taking it apart, so you can put it back together again.

REMOVING SOMETHING FROM A SHAFT

Use screwdrivers, or what ever fits to gently pry the part off. Often the part is really stuck, and a gear, or bearing puller will be needed. They are fairly inexpensive, but can also be rented. Search for "equipment rental," or "rental services."

See: **Tip 78**, removing something from a shaft.

140 ▷ SPLITTING A HOUSING

Often, after removing all the bolts that hold two halves of a machine together, it will not come apart.

You can persuade it with two or three screwdrivers. Tap them gently into the gasket between the two halves, at several places. Keep taping until it comes apart.

If it does not want to move, look for the screw or bolt you missed.

Cutting oil

Metal surface

Wood back up board

DRILLING HOLES IN METAL

141 TIP

Make an indentation, in the metal, with a punch. This will keep the drill bit in place when you first start.

Go slow. Get a variable speed 3/8 drill, and good quality drill bits for steel, and some cutting oil. Let the drill bit cut the metal, rather than trying to wear a hole in it. Apply cutting oil at the contact point. If it smokes a lot, you are going too fast.

If you are drilling larger holes, get a ½ inch drill. If precision is called for, buy a table mounted drill press. See: **Tip 119**, about cheap tools.

Hang on tight when the drill bit goes through the bottom of the hole, the drill will jerk.

Put a piece of wood under the piece of metal to make a clean exit wound.

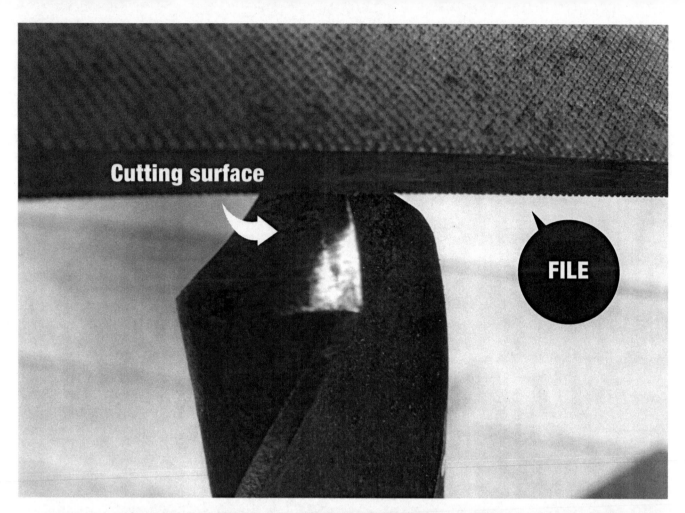

Cutting surface

FILE

142   SHARPENING THINGS

Look closely at scissors, knives, your blender blade, you will see the tapered cutting surface.

A larger drill bit may be worth sharpening.

Use a grinding wheel, or a fine metal file, and restore the cutting surfaces. Push the file along the surface away from you. Do not file on the back stroke.

An axe file, or flat chain saw file will sharpen most home and garden tools with a blade. Just find the cutting surface, use the file, or grinder to restore its original shape. It is really easy.

Tighten the blades on scissors by compressing the rivet with a hammer. See: **Tip 63**, sharpening scissors.

The best way to keep kitchen knives sharp is to use a steel. The steel has super fine grooves on it

that will sharpen knife blades. Hold the steel in one hand; bring the blade down it, towards you. Sharpen on the down stroke. Repeat on the other side. The blade should be held at an angle to the steel, on both strokes.

It takes lots of practice, but will produce the sharpest knives possible. Test the sharpness by dragging your thumb across the blade (NOT down the blade, which will cut you). Increasing friction means the blade is getting sharper.

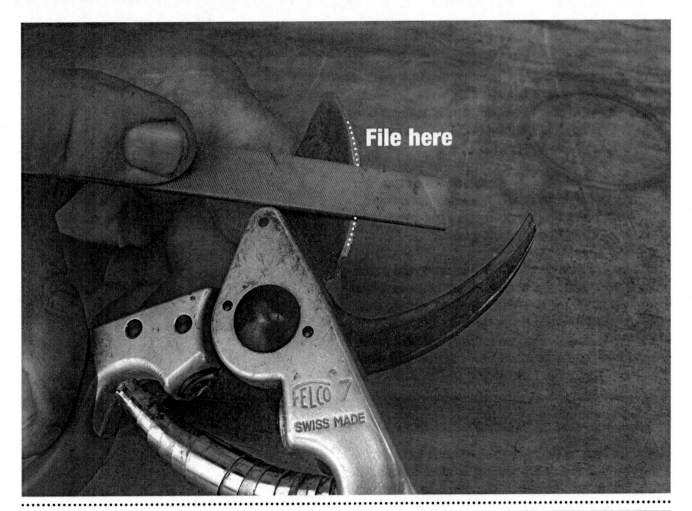

File here

Sharpen one side

There are either two or three wires inside the cord of an electrical tool. If the tool has a plastic body, usually there are only two wires, one black and one white. If the tool has a metal body, then there are three: black, white, and green.

The black is "hot" although the white can be too. You can get a shock from either. The green is "ground." Things will work fine if you mix up the black and white, but DO NOT mix up the green.

Inside the tool the green wire attaches to the metal body. If the current escapes from the black or white wires, (a short) it will go to ground, rather than through you. If there is no metal body, and the body of the tool is plastic, there will usually not be a green ground wire, because plastic will not conduct electricity into you.

The shaft has to be held so it will not turn. There are several tricks. If something is attached to the shaft, like a lawnmower blade, use it for leverage. (See: **Safety**)

A long screwdriver shoved through something like cooling fins, will work. But be careful, aluminum fins will break.

Use a vise, vice grips, channel lock pliers, cloth wrench, or weld a piece onto the shaft to use as a lever. Some machines have special slots or holes to put a pin, or screwdriver blade into, to prevent the shaft from turning.

Last resort, use a chisel to cut the nut, or turn it.

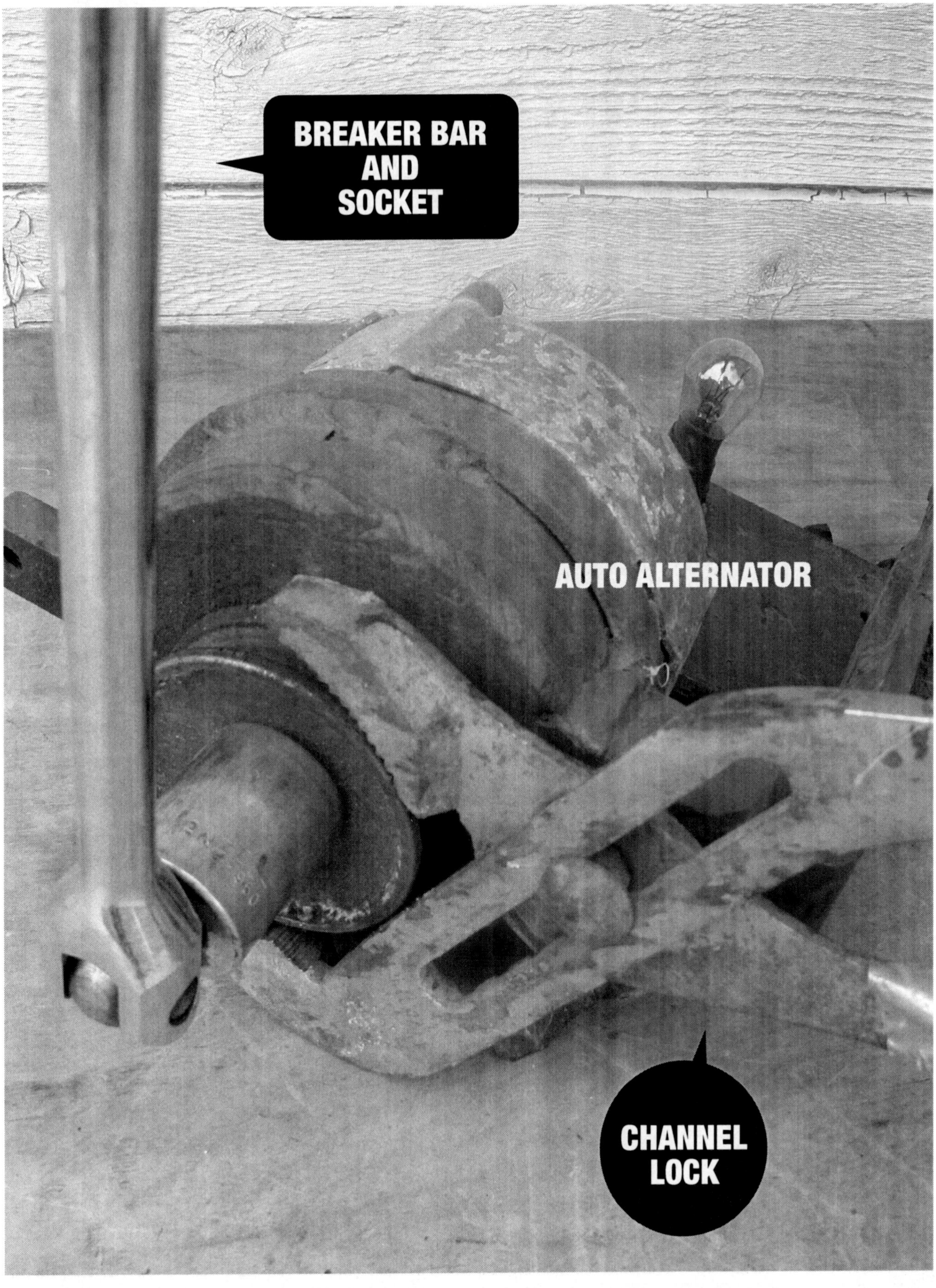
BREAKER BAR AND SOCKET
AUTO ALTERNATOR
CHANNEL LOCK

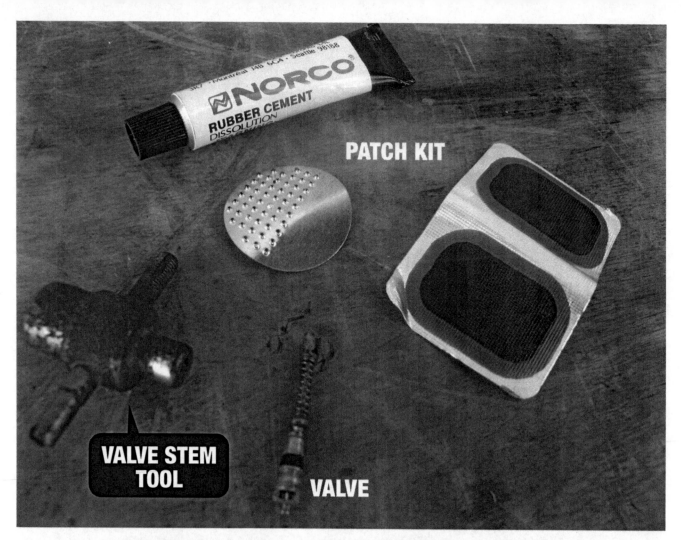

PATCH KIT

VALVE STEM
TOOL

VALVE

TIP | 145 | FIXING A FLAT TIRE

Tubeless. Go buy a repair kit, and follow the directions, or better yet, put a tube in it.

All the tubeless tires, like on wheelbarrows, and hand trucks, that I have gotten lately (made in China) have deflated promptly. The only cure, is a tube.

Tube tire: First inflate the tube, before you take it out of the tire. Put some spit on the end of the valve stem, see if any bubbles form. If they do, get a valve stem tool, and tighten it, or replace it.

I never had a problem with valve stems until the Chinese started making them.

If it still leaks you will need to remove the tube, and patch it with a kit from a bike shop, or hardware store.

Take the tire half way off, using two screwdrivers. Take the tube out. Blow it up, put the inflated tube in water to find the leak.

Look closely, you will see a little stream of bubbles. If you do not see them, inflate more.

Get a patch kit, and patch it. Before you put it back in, check the inside of the tire to see if whatever caused the hole in the tube is still there. Make sure the valve stem goes into the rim the way it came out.

Push tire here

Pull tube out

Stretch tire back on

DREMEL

146 ▷ PLASTIC HOUSINGS

Many machine units are encased in plastic housings. These things appear to be impossible to take apart. If there is a seam, it can be taken apart. (Obviously it was not born, it was assembled).

You may have to break a corner to see how it works, but so what? It was not working when you started, and you can always fix the breaks. See: **Tip 124**, bungee cords and duct tape. See: **Tip 68**, breaking things.

You can use a small grinder like a Dremel tool to cut into the plastic in a neat way.

Once you get inside the plastic, the place to start is loose, broken or dirty electrical connections.

See: **Tip 70**, appliance electrical problems.

NEVER work on a household appliance without unplugging it. AC current (what comes out of the wall) can KILL you.

Trying to get inside plastic housings on cars is the subject of another book. There are many ways that screw heads, latching devices, and other parts are concealed behind plastic. See: **Tip 50** for some solutions to auto plastic housing problems.

Must be equally smooth
(this needs more work)

Small items, like an aluminum lawn mower cylinder head can be made flat again, with the following procedure.

Go find a piece of really thick plate glass. ½ inch or larger. Check with glass shops.
Put a piece of emory cloth, or sand paper, on the glass. Place the glass on a hard, flat surface.

Rub the part, lightly, over the emory cloth. Watch the progress on the side you are smoothing. When all the sides and corners are of an equal sheen, or smoothness, you have succeeded.

Adjustable hose clamp

TIP **148** ▷ **YOUR OWN METAL FABRICATION SHOP**

One of the earliest things my father taught me was that I could fabricate anything out of aluminum. It is soft, pliable, and strong. You can cut it, pound it, drill it, and bend it to almost any shape. Airplanes are made out of it.

You should have a collection of aluminum plate, in different thicknesses. Making all sorts of things with aluminum is easy.

Check out the metal recyclers in your city. They have tons of metal, at bargain prices.

You can never have too much aluminum plate, and metal odds and ends around.

Make drip holes with a nail

This will save money, and it sure makes painting cleaner. If you are, like me, a really messy painter, it will save you hiring people to scrape paint drips from your trendy bamboo floor.

After you open that can of paint, fix the can by punching holes in the little trough where the lid fits. Use a small nail.

Then, as you wipe your brush, the paint flows back into the can. The lid will still seal perfectly.

There is another savings. If the groove gets full of paint, the lid will not seal properly. If air gets to the paint, it will harden, and it will look like the whole can should be thrown away.

Cut paint scum loose

Dispose of scum

150 SAVE A CAN OF PAINT

When air gets to the paint inside a can, it does exactly what it is supposed to do. It dries.

If you get a good seal on the paint can, it will not be exposed to the air.

Once a scum develops on the top of the paint, it needs to be removed, before you can use what is left in the can. Cut around the edge with a knife, and lift the whole thing out, and throw it away. The paint that is left is perfectly good, and just needs to be stirred.

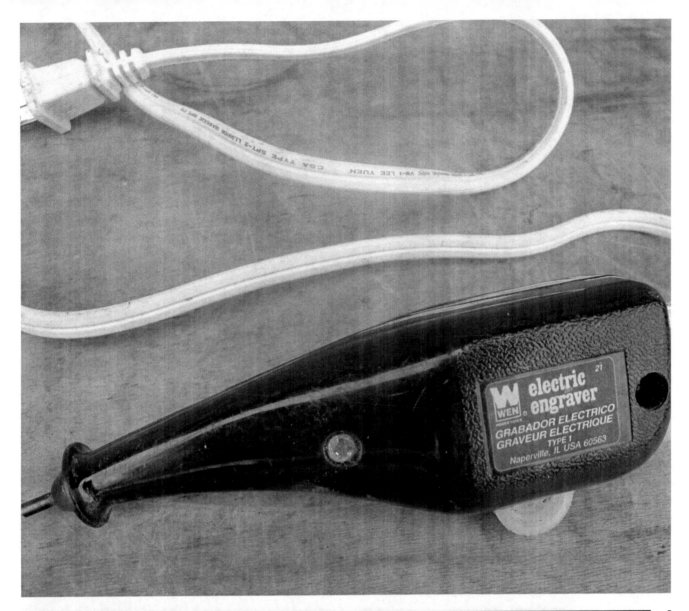

Chainsaws, tools, bicycles and electronics top the list of things that thieves take. That is why there are so many of each in pawn shops.

You stand a small chance of getting your tools back, if you buy a tool engraver, put your initials, and driver's license number on each tool. Cops have instant access to your driver's license number, but not to your Social Security, or Social Insurance Number.

I once got a whole toolbox full of tools back, because I engraved everything.

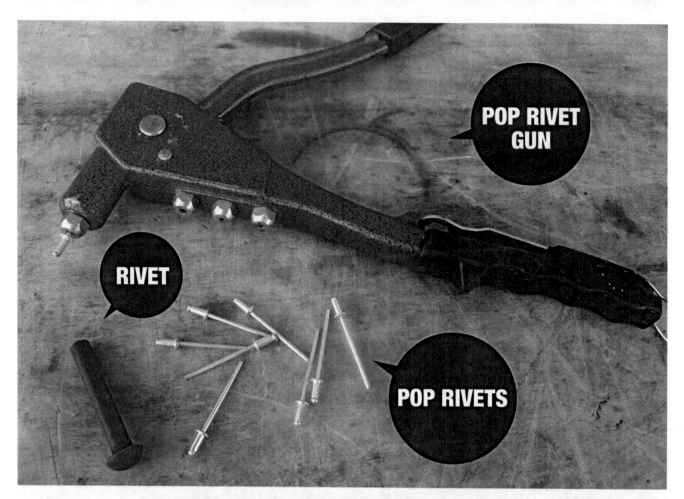

POP RIVET GUN

RIVET

POP RIVETS

152 ▷ RIVETS

There are two kinds, pop, and standard. They are used to hold metal things together.

When you buy pop rivets, the package should tell you how big a hole to drill. Just make the hole a hair bigger than the rivet.

Use the pop rivet gun to insert the rivet. Usually you need to squeeze the handle once, then move the stem of the rivet further into the gun, and squeeze until the stem breaks. Practice makes perfect.

Regular rivets need a hole just a hair bigger than the shaft. When inserted, flatten one end with a ball peen hammer.

See: **Tip 63**, sharpening scissors.

153 ▷ SHEET METAL SCREWS

Faster than rivets, but a bit tricky. Drill a very small hole in both pieces of very thin metal. Make a bigger hole in thicker metal.

You can use the heel of your hand to drive the screw in before trying to twist it. See: **Tip 10**, the hand.

When the screw is properly installed, the tip will just be visible where it comes through the second piece, only two complete threads need come through.

Most short wood screws can be used for sheet metal.

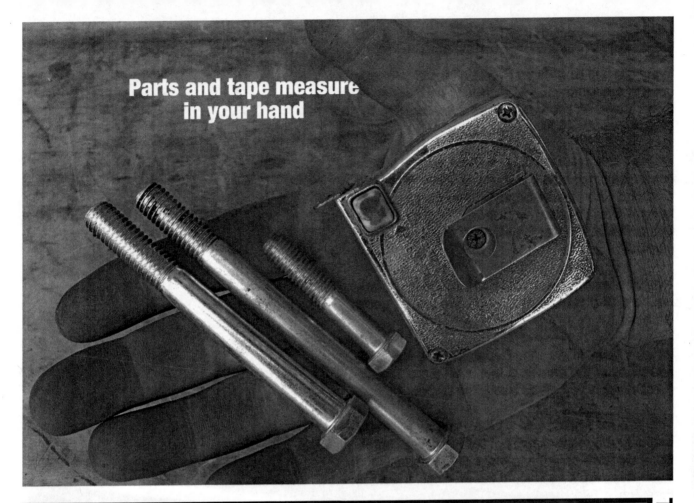
Parts and tape measure
in your hand

BUYING PARTS 154 TIP

Always go to the hardware store with the old part in your hand, or with a tape measure to check the dimensions of the item you want.

Nuts and bolts are available at most hardware stores. Get the same grade, or the next higher one. See: **Tip 102**, about grades of hardware.

You can also get o-rings, special washers, and fittings, couplings, rivets, cotter pins, nails, and screws, at most big hardware stores.

Except for those special washers, fittings, etc, you will have to buy a package of 4, 6 or more. Buy a few more than you need, and start your own hardware store.

Get a selection of wood/metal screws, nuts and bolts, so you do not have to take the car into town,

just for one 50 cent item. And at today's gas prices that sounds OK.

Put your stock of parts in the bottom half of milk cartons. They are just the right size.

THE FREE STORE

Every city has landfills that contain tons of perfectly good things. Unfortunately, there is no way for people to get them. As soon as you put something on the curb, it becomes trash.

Where I live, we have a Free Store, where usable goods are dropped off, and you can shop for free. It is staffed with volunteers. They keep the place tidy, hang clothes on racks, organize the books and CDs that come in, display the working appliances, and give useful advice

The store contains every imaginable consumer product, lots of bicycles, and parts, and lots of good clothes.

We also have a Recycling Depot. Metal is recycled, and many of the photos in this book are of broken items dropped off at the Recycling Depot.

This is a rural area, and we have to pay for every bag of garbage we drop off at the Recycling Depot. But if we have something that still has some life in it, we can drop it for free, at the Free Store. So it is Free Times Two.

Why not approach some charity in your town to set up a Free Store. Or talk to your local town counselor. Make it easy for goods to have a second life.

Don't be surprised if you encounter incredible resistance on this. The entire supply chain of stuff from China, and elsewhere just HATES the idea of free stuff.

PRODUCTS AND BRANDS

Any products or brand names mentioned in this book were mentioned because I have used those products or brands, and think they are worth using.

This book is not a commercial message dressed up as helpful advice, as is so common on the internet.

I have not received any compensation from anyone for mentioning anything. Not even a bottle of wine.

INDEX

BY TIP NUMBER UNLESS OTHERWISE STATED

T

U

V

W

Y

Lawrence Pierce grew up in Missouri and Texas and currently lives with his partner of 11 years, Margit Lieder, on Hornby Island, BC.

His career of fixing things started at age 9, and continued through high school, with a variety of English sports cars, which needed constant attention. During the late 1960s he lived in San Francisco, and was a mechanic at a Volkswagen dealership in the East Bay.

During the 70's he tried farming, without much success, except to learn more about fixing his machinery, which constantly broke down.

The summer of 1982 found him in Whitehorse, Yukon, repairing any vehicle that got that far on the Alaska Highway.

During the last 23 years, he spent his weekends fixing things, and renovating several houses. During the day, he was a litigation lawyer in downtown Vancouver, specializing in personal injury and disability insurance claims, representing people denied by insurance companies.

He is now an organic farmer, with a small vineyard, and 3 acres of blueberries. He grows grapes, makes wine, runs the winery, and fixes things.